CURRENTS

AUTHORS

Jo M. Stanchfield

Thomas G. Gunning

Houghton Mifflin Company   BOSTON

Atlanta   Dallas   Geneva, Illinois   Hopewell, New Jersey   Palo Alto   Toronto

Acknowledgments

For each of the selections listed below, grateful acknowledgment is made for permission to adapt and/or reprint original copyrighted material, as follows:

"Flying Messengers," abridged and simplified from "Typesetting Over Boston," by Paul Langner, in *The Boston Globe*, October 24, 1982. Reprinted courtesy of The Boston Globe.

"Foul Shot," by Edwin A. Hoey. Reprinted by permission of *Read* Magazine, published by Xerox Education Publications, © 1962, Xerox Corp.

"The Golden Knights," by Jan W. Steenblik, published originally in *Boys' Life* Magazine, June 1981. By permission of the author.

"Gorilla Showdown," abridged and adapted from pp. 37–42 in *Zoo Vet*, by David C. Taylor (J.B. Lippincott). Copyright © 1976, 1977 by David C. Taylor. Reprinted by permission of the publishers, Harper & Row, Publishers, Inc. and George Allen & Unwin (Publishers) Ltd.

"The History of Roller Coasters," by Barbara Seuling, © 1983 Children's Television Workshop. Used by permission of Children's Television Workshop.

"Never shall I leave . . . ," from *Hollering Sun*, by Nancy Wood. Text copyright © 1972 by Nancy Wood. Used by permission of the author.

"Sam's Choice," adapted from *Run, Don't Walk*, by Harriet Savitz. Copyright © 1979 by Harriet Savitz. Used by permission of Franklin Watts, Inc.

Acknowledgments and Art Credits are continued on page 240.

Contents

They were fast. They were hot. They were
the Skate Patrol, and they had a job to do.

The Skate Patrol

by Eve Bunting

James and Milton skated through the park. Their
wheels hummed on the path. It was cool under the
trees. They streaked past the bench where the Mystery Man sat. Sun glinted on his bald head and
glasses.

"Zoom! Zoom!" James held his arms wide,
swooping, flying. The Mystery Man pulled his feet
out of the way.

"Hey!" A park worker shook his rake at the boys.
"No skating in the park! Roll on out of here!"

"Oh, man!" James made a face.

"Let's try the path around your apartment again," Milton said as they skated across the street. "That was the best place ever for skating. All those good, hairy curves and that nice, smooth concrete."

"We can't," James said. "Mrs. Grump's watching, like always." They stared up at Mrs. Grump's apartment window. And sure enough, there she was, frowning! Probably getting ready to tell James's mom if they did anything wrong.

"I bet she thinks we'd knock her over or some-thing," Milton muttered. "Your mom's too nice to her."

"Mom has to be nice," James said. "She has to be nice to Mrs. Grump and all the tenants." James used to think his mom owned the apartments, but she just took care of them. That way, she and James got to live in Apartment A for free.

Milton poked James in the ribs. "The Mystery Man is still there," he said.

James looked across at the park. The Mystery Man's bench was half hidden by the bushes.

"Do you think he's in love with Mrs. Grump?" asked Milton. "Maybe that's why he sits there every day, watching the apartments."

"Milt," James said. He felt weird all of a sudden. "Milt?" he asked. "Did you hear what you just said?"

"What? What did I say?"

"The M.M.'s watching our apartment house. Who lives in our apartment house? Me and Mom and a bunch of old people. And we've got more single old ladies than anyone else. Do you remember the Creep Thief — the guy who goes around grabbing old ladies' purses? He struck Holly Street last week. That's not far from here."

"You mean *he's* the Creep Thief?" Milton whispered. "We better call the police. We could sneak over to the park and watch him till they get here."

"Wait!" James said. "What if we caught him in the act? What if we saved someone, even Mrs. Grump? I bet she'd let us skate anywhere we wanted! We'll need a good stakeout, though — where we can watch *his* stakeout. Somewhere in the park."

"Will we take our skates?"

"For sure. We may have to move fast."

"Wow!" Milton said. "You know what we are, James? The Skate Patrol. Look out, Creep Thief, here we come!"

A good stakeout spot was hard to find. It had to be a place where they could see the M.M., but where the M.M. couldn't see them.

"Come on, Milt," James said. He led the way to the men's bathroom. Inside, there was a high window. They took turns standing on the sink, peering out. But nothing happened all afternoon. By 6:00, the M.M. had left the park. The S.P. (Skate Patrol) left, too.

The next day the Skate Patrol staked out again and waited—and waited. Finally, Mrs. Grump came out of the apartment building.

"Hey, here she comes!" James said.

Mrs. Grump came down the apartment steps, holding her big, black purse. First she peered up and down the street. Then she headed for Eddie's Market. The M.M. got on her trail fast. The S.P. slunk behind him, on foot.

Mrs. Grump pushed open Eddie's door. The M.M. went into the market after her. The S.P. leaned on Eddie's outside wall. James loosened his laces so he would be ready.

A scream startled James and Milton. It came from inside the market. James swallowed nervously. It had been a kind of game up to now. But it wasn't anymore. "Come on," he croaked.

Milton didn't move.

"Come *on*," James said again. Together they crashed through Eddie's door.

Eddie was standing behind his meat counter. He looked as though he might pass out. Mrs. Grump was sitting on the floor by the back door.

"Hey, what happened?" asked James.

"The Creep robbed me," Mrs. Grump said. "But I got him on the side of the head with an apple. I'm still a pretty good shot."

James ran to the back door. The M.M. was dashing across the parking lot.

"Quick, Milton!" James yelled. "After him!"

They laced their skates and took off across the parking lot. The M.M. was racing around the corner. He was really moving. But James was moving faster. He was fire. He was lightning. He was gaining. Milton thundered right behind him. The Skate Patrol was hot — H-O-T.

They were on the sidewalk now. James could hear the M.M. panting. James crouched. Crash! He hit the M.M. low in the legs. They fell together into a pile of raked-up leaves.

"What are you doing, you crazy kid?" the M.M. wheezed. He was struggling hard.

"Milt, quick — call the cops," James gasped.

With one heave, the M.M. pushed James off and was on his feet. "I *am* a cop, you dummy. I'm chasing *him*."

James looked to the place where he pointed and saw another man running ahead. There was something in his hand — a large, black purse.

"Oh, no." James looked up from where he was sprawled on the sidewalk. "Honest, you're a cop?"

But the M.M. was already running again. Milton pulled James up and steadied him, and they were off.

They speed-rode side by side. They caught up with the M.M. and passed him by. James's wheels jumped the curb — a perfect landing. The thief was yanking at the door of a blue van, but the Skate Patrol was on him. They hit the Creep Thief together. He crashed against the van and bounced back into the street. James sat on his head. Milton lay across his feet.

"Hey, this must be some kind of mistake. Just let me up, kid."

"Quiet, Creep Thief," Milton said.

The M.M. jogged up to them. He was puffing hard.

"You should get yourself skates," James told him. He and Milton got up. James swooped up Mrs. Grump's purse.

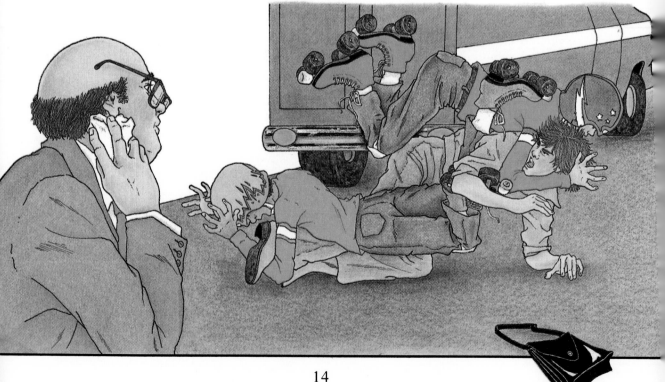

The M.M. put handcuffs on the Creep Thief. "I'm Officer Meeks," he said. "Ten of us have been staked out around here, watching places where older ladies live. Say, aren't you the two kids who like to hang out all the time in the bathroom in the park?"

Milton looked at James. James shrugged and grinned.

Back at Eddie's, Officer Meeks handcuffed the thief to the dairy case. Then he went to use Eddie's phone. Mrs. Grump was sitting on Eddie's stool, sipping tea from a mug.

"I got your purse, Mrs. Grump," James said. "Are you hurt?"

"No," Mrs. Grump said. "The thief came in the back door and pushed me from behind. If I'd seen him, I bet I could have handled him." She pointed to the Creep Thief. "See that bump on his head? That's where I got him with an apple. I used to pitch for a softball team."

James grinned. "You *are* a good shot, Mrs. Grump." Mrs. Grump wasn't the way he thought she'd be. But then, who was?

"Crump," Mrs. Grump said. "That's my name — not Grump. You boys used to skate outside the apartments a lot, didn't you?" Mrs. Crump said.

"Sure," Milton said. "Till you complained to James's mom."

"Why don't you put your foot in your mouth, Milton?" James said fiercely.

Mrs. Crump held up her hand. "The truth's the truth. But now, see what's happened? If it weren't for you, I would have lost my purse. You know, I would feel a lot safer with you boys patrolling outside my apartment again." Mrs. Crump smiled. "And I'll talk to your mother, James."

Officer Meeks came back with his notebook. "Now Mrs. Grump . . . " he began.

"Her name is not Grump, it's Crump," James said. "Mrs. CRUMP."

FOLLOW-UP

1. Why is the Skate Patrol a good name for James and Milton?

2. James and Milton thought that no one else knew about their stakeout. What sentence on page 15 shows that they were wrong?

3. How had James's feelings about Mrs. Crump changed at the end of the story?

Could Bud come up with something crazy
and win this race?

Water Bed Off the Starboard Bow

by A.R. Swinnerton

A boatless boat race doesn't sound like much, but I talked myself into entering. The half-mile river race was held by the local merchants. Any kid who was thirteen years old or younger could enter. Anything could be used, as long as it wasn't a real boat. It could be paddled, sailed, poled, or rowed by no more than two kids.

I paid my five-dollar fee and made up my mind to win. The question was, How? I decided to stop by to see what the Snyder twins were up to. But they had their garage door shut, and the windows were papered over.

Molly answered the door. Or it could have been Polly, for all I could tell. "Get lost," she said. "Work on your own thing. We got ours." She slammed the door shut when I reminded her that friends were for sharing. Whatever they had going, I was sure it was something pretty sharp.

That's when I remembered that my grandmother has her own museum. She never throws anything away. I drifted over there and cut her grass, just to be on the safe side. Then I wandered out to her old stable. That's where she stores her junk. I poked around, raising the dust and waving at cobwebs. Then I spotted this thing under an old buggy.

No question about it, it was for a kid. The four spoked wheels were rusted and busted. There was a wooden seat and a lever sticking up toward the front. The lever had a handle on it.

"What is it?" I asked Grandma.

She gave it a kick. "That old thing. I think it's called an Irish Mail. It belonged to your grandfather. Or to his grandfather. You sit on the seat and pump that handle and it drives the rear wheels, or so they say. You can take it home, Bud. But only if you say you'll never bring it back."

Pop helped me take it home in the car. We were standing there, staring at it, when my little sister, Dimwit, joined us. Her real name is Perry. She's a pest. I only call her Perry when I need a favor.

She kicked it, just like Grandma. "It'll never get off the ground," she said. "Can I ask what it is?"

"No!" I said.

"Bud," Pop warned.

"She bugs me," I said. "I can't think when she's around."

"Can't think at all," she said, skipping away. "Anyway," she yelled back, "I know what the Snyder twins are making, and you don't."

It took me a whole day to clean my contraption. When I finished, I set it up on blocks and tried it out.

I could turn the rear axle and wheels by pumping the handle. OK, I had a way to make it go. Now I needed something to float it on.

Behind the garage was the old box that Pop mixed cement in. It was about four feet wide and six feet long. Both ends slanted out, and the sides were about ten inches high. Pop helped me put it in the garage.

When I had chipped away the loose cement, I flushed out the box with water. Then I painted it inside and out with some blacktop coating. That would waterproof it.

"Now I'm stuck," I said to Pop. "The handle will pump and turn the rear axle. But I need to rebuild it so that it will turn a propeller behind the boat."

"Too hard," he grunted. "Why not fasten paddle wheels on the ends of the axle?"

That made sense. "Won't the water leak in where the axle goes through the sides of the box, though?" I asked.

"Yep," said Pop. "You'll need to pack around it."

I made two paddle wheels out of plywood. I fastened them to the axle. Then I followed Pop's suggestions for packing. "OK," I said, staring at the thing. "Now how will I steer it?"

Perry had come up behind us. She had that know-it-all look on her face. "I'll tell you how," she said. "And I'll tell you what the Snyder twins are making,

if you let me ride along. Fifty-fifty split on the prize money."

I glanced at Pop. "Won't hurt to listen," he said.

"All right, then," Perry said. "I'll jump around from side to side so one paddle digs deeper. And I'll yell so much the others will get jumpy."

Pop and I both had to laugh. "What about the Snyders?" I asked.

"I peeked in," she said. "It's a bed. A floating four-poster bed with a canopy. The way it looked, they could use the canopy as a sail."

Pop and I roared.

"Don't forget," said Perry. "I'm your first mate."

I strapped six empty one-gallon cans to the sides of our boat. I hoped the cans would keep it from tipping in the water. Then we took the boat down to the river and launched it. It was a little low in the water, but it made headway when I pumped the handle. Some water seeped in around the packing, but not much.

Pop cheered and Perry yelled. I held up my thumbs. "Victory at sea!" I shouted. "Full speed ahead!"

It was a sight at the starting line on the afternoon of the race. On the shore and in the water were all kinds of crazy boats. I counted four bathtubs with floats, a few log rafts, and a boat made from two oil drums lashed together. There was even an old baby crib that was waterproofed with plastic sheeting. And there in the water, tugging at its lines, was the Snyders' bed.

When everyone was lined up, the judges checked us for life jackets. They warned us about ramming. Then the gun sounded. "Pump!" Perry screamed.

We were moving down the river, under a bridge solidly lined with people. They were all cheering and screaming as if it were the Olympics.

"Watch it!" I yelled at Perry. "Lean starboard, not port."

She stamped her foot. "Say right or left," she screamed. "I'm all mixed up!"

"Right! Watch the bathtub. Push it away before we ram it!" I shouted.

"You just keep on pumping. The oil drums are gaining, Bud!" cried Perry. The bathtub tipped over just as we passed the crib.

"Where's the bed?" I yelled.

She pointed. "Up there. The bed's ahead, Bud. The bed is winning! Move over! I'll help you pump."

She crowded beside me. All four of our hands were on the pump. We were gaining, but slowly. Panting, I looked up. "Look!" I yelled.

A sudden breeze had rippled across the water and caught the bed's canopy. It rose up and gave a sharp, flapping sound. Then it sailed free like a loose kite. The bed was dead in the water.

We put our heads down and pumped. We closed in on the bed and inched ahead. "We're swamping!" yelled Perry. "Look!"

Water was gushing in around the axle. "Jump out!" I shouted. "It isn't deep. I'm stronger—I'll pump."

"But I'm lighter," she said. "Jump off the back, Bud, and give us a push!"

24

No time to argue. I jumped, pushing off as hard as I could. Still pumping like mad, Perry crossed the finish line. Only the handle, her head, and her arms were still above the water!

There was a lot of cheering and backslapping. Then we were in the winner's circle, soaking wet. Perry grabbed the check and grinned. "I forgot to mention something," she said. "I'm also the banker."

Sure, we had our little disagreements after that. But I never called her Dimwit again. It just didn't seem to fit.

FOLLOW-UP

1. What did Bud use to make his contraption?

2. How did Bud feel about Perry *before* the race? How did he feel about Perry *after* the race?

3. Who was really in command on the boat — Bud or Perry? Why do you think that?

There was nothing special about the
Mary Rose — until it sank.

Twice-Sunk Gold

by Linda Hirschmann

Workers along the Boston docks sniffed the salty
air. They looked up to read the early morning sky. It
was a calm morning, with a sunny day ahead. No one
had a hint of what would soon happen.

July 27, 1640, began as usual. The ferry was running that Monday. Many ships bobbed in the harbor.
Outbound ships were waiting to be loaded. Other
ships waited for workers to unload their cargo and
row it to shore.

"Room ahead!" shouted the carriers. They were
bent under the weight of chests and bales. They stag-
gered across the docks and into the streets without
looking. "Make way!" they cried.

Bendall's Dock was swarming with people. Edward
Bendall was in charge of the ferry and the barges
that loaded up the big ships. He seemed to be everywhere, hiring workers and shouting orders. Workers

jammed the dock. When fourteen crew members from the merchant ship *Mary Rose* rowed in, they had to push for space to step ashore.

Around one in the afternoon, the waterfront finally settled down. At that hour, the people of Boston usually returned home for a quiet meal. This day would be different, however. As they ate their dinner, they heard a loud, crashing BOOM.

What had happened? For miles around, people stared fearfully at their shaking ceilings and walls. "An earthquake!" some thought. But when they rushed outside, they saw flames in the harbor.

The *Mary Rose* had exploded and was burning. Shattered boards floated about the harbor. The rest of the ship quickly sank. Rowers pushed off to look for anyone who might have survived. Although the boats went all over the harbor area, the searchers rescued only one man. They discovered him dazed and clinging to the door of a hatchway. No one else was found alive.

What had sunk the *Mary Rose*? Fourteen people thought they knew. They were the lucky crew members who had rowed ashore that morning. They knew that the *Mary Rose* had carried ten cannons and twenty-one kegs of gunpowder. It must have been someone with a candle, they guessed. Someone who was too careless, too near those kegs of gunpowder.

There was a story that the ship had also been carrying gold and silver coins. One of the crew said that the captain of the *Mary Rose* had hidden the coins inside a cannon. Few people believed him.

Throughout Boston, people were shocked by the loss of the *Mary Rose* and her crew. They wondered about the lost gold. And they talked about the problem of the wrecked ship. A ship sunk in a busy harbor meant trouble. If other ships rammed the wreck, they also could go down.

The *Mary Rose* had to be removed. The leaders of Boston chose Edward Bendall to do the job. They set the terms. Bendall would have two years. If he could clear the harbor, he would own everything that was brought up. But if he removed only part of the wreck, he could keep only half of it.

The work would be dangerous. For one thing, few people in 1640 knew how to swim. But Edward Bendall had a plan. He would build a wooden diving tub. He would bring up the *Mary Rose,* piece by piece. Some people didn't believe his plan would work. Others weren't sure what to think.

Bendall made his plans quickly. But he built and tested his tub slowly, carefully. The bottom of the tub was open, and the top was closed. Weights were hung from the bottom to make the tub sink. Chains were attached to its top so it could be linked to a barge up above.

Inside the tub, Bendall would sit on a platform. His head would be in the air trapped at the top. His feet would dangle in the water. Two ropes would hang nearby. By tugging one, he could tell the men in the barge to pull him forward. A tug on the other rope would mean to pull him up.

Crowds mobbed the waterfront the day Bendall made his first dive. No one was surprised when the tub sank. But they were amazed when Bendall came up after half an hour. He was alive! The tub worked!

Finding the wreck was easy. But it took weeks of work to raise the pieces. The hull of the ship came first. Then came masts, hunks of deck, cannons, kettles, and chests.

Where was the gold? Excitement spread whenever a piece of the wreck was checked. But not one coin was found. The cannons were checked. Nine held nothing. But the barrel of the last one was jammed with cording. Was the cording there to guard something crammed deep inside?

A man tugged at the cording. He was unable to budge it. "Heavy as lead, it is," he grunted.

"Little wonder," said another. "For nearly two years it has soaked up salt water."

Straining, the workers yanked out the cording. When it fell free, the cannon was empty. "That shows the worth of gossip," people agreed. "The poorest of ships, once it is sunk, is said to be rich with gold."

Before he did anything else, Bendall wanted to test the cannons. They were his to sell, since he had cleared the harbor. They would bring him more money if they still worked.

Workers rolled a keg of gunpowder to the dock. They didn't dare shoot a cannon ball into the crowded harbor. Instead, they crammed the cording back down the barrel of the cannon.

A flame was struck. The powder flashed. The cannon boomed. Cording sailed into the air, high over the harbor. A glittering rain fell from it.

"Silver! Gold!" the crowd cried. Salt water had not weighed down that cording. It had been heavy with coins, *hundreds* of coins. They had been hidden inside the braids of cording!

At the next low tide, people who strolled near the water found silver and gold coins. They kept the coins—until Bendall went to court. The judge ruled that the coins were his. But when the coins were collected, they made only a tiny pile.

This is a true telling of the facts about Edward Bendall and the twice-sunk gold. It is a strange tale. But stranger than the tale itself is this: Although many people know where that gold sank, no one else has ever tried to bring it up. And even though Bendall was daring and clever, he tried only once.

In the silt and muck of Boston harbor—somewhere—lies a treasure of gold and silver. It is still waiting to be found.

FOLLOW-UP

1. This story is called "Twice-Sunk Gold." How did the gold sink twice?

2. The people of Boston were interested in the *Mary Rose* for two reasons. What were those reasons?

3. Why did Bendall have the cannon fired?

There was one gold miner in the 1800's who was different from all the others.

Miners' Angel

"Gold!" At that cry, eager gold-seekers swarmed into the West in the late 1800's. Everyone had the same hope — to get rich quick.

Wherever the gold-seekers went, "boom towns" sprang up almost overnight. These towns were built by people who followed the miners. Hotels and eating places went up quickly. Prices were sky-high because gold was so plentiful. In one boom town, eggs sold for a dollar apiece! Everyone wanted to make easy money.

Well, not quite everyone. There was one who was different. Nellie Cashman was both a miner and a hotel owner. Nellie loved prospecting. If there was a gold or silver strike anywhere out West, Nellie was sure to show up. She spent fifty years out West and made a lot of money. But Nellie was not greedy. In fact, she gave away most of her money to people who really needed it.

Nellie was greatly admired by her fellow miners, for many reasons. She could match some of the best miners in skill. She was tough and fearless, but she was also kind. Everyone knew that Nellie Cashman gave food and shelter to miners who weren't lucky. They were thankful for her kindness. The miners gave her names such as Miners' Angel, Angel of Tombstone (Arizona), and Saint of the Sourdoughs.

Nellie's daring life as a miner really began in 1874. In that year, she joined the gold rush north to Dease Lake in British Columbia, Canada. At the time, Nellie was only about twenty-three years old. She made money not only by prospecting but also by running a hotel for the miners at Dease Lake.

After a while, Nellie left Dease Lake and went south. Then one day she heard that many of the miners at Dease Lake were very sick. At once, she collected 1,500 pounds of food and supplies. She hired a crew of six to go with her. She set out for Dease Lake again.

It was a hard trip. Using showshoes and sleds, Nellie and her group braved the cold and the snow. One night a snowslide roared into their camp. The snow swept Nellie—and her tent—down a hill. She had to dig herself out. Nellie and her party finally made it to Dease Lake, and Nellie treated the sick miners successfully.

Then, in 1880, Nellie heard about a rich silver strike in Arizona. So she set out for the boom town of Tombstone. There she bought an old building, the Russ House, and made it into a hotel. Nellie had a good head for the hotel business. Soon people were saying that her hotel served the best meals in town.

By 1883, Nellie's Tombstone hotel business was booming. But when she got word that there was gold

Tombstone, Arizona, about 1880

in Baja California, she was off again. Along with twenty-one other miners, Nellie started out across the desert. After a while, the party's water was almost gone. They hadn't found any gold, and they were lost in the middle of a burning desert. Nellie knew they couldn't last long. Because she was in better shape than the others, Nellie went for help — alone. Luckily, she soon reached a settlement. With Nellie guiding them, a rescue team brought back goatskins filled with water.

That would have been quite enough to unnerve most people, but not Nellie Cashman. She kept on prospecting. She traveled as far north as the Klondike in the wilds of the Canadian northwest. By dogsled and on snowshoes, Nellie went on seeking and finding gold.

Nellie stayed on in the Canadian north. She owned and ran mines, eating places, and food stores. But Nellie was never one to stay put for long. She even drove a dog-sled team across 750 miles of unexplored land in Alaska. By that time, Nellie Cashman was close to 70 years old!

The Search

by Shel Silverstein

I went to find the pot of gold
That's waiting where the rainbow ends.
I searched and searched and searched and searched
And searched and searched, and then—
There it was, deep in the grass,
Under an old and twisty bough.
It's mine, it's mine, it's mine at last. . . .
What do I search for now?

Terry knew that helping her dad would be hard work. But she never thought it would almost kill her.

The Wreck of the Sea Angel

by Steven Ratiner

The first time I asked Dad was when I was twelve years old.

"Too young," he told me. "I wouldn't take you out on the *Sea Angel* just for the fun of it. Fishing is hard work, Terry, and it could be dangerous."

So I waited. I asked him again when I was fourteen. Dad seemed surprised when I brought it up. But he smiled, too.

"Too skinny," he finally answered. "I can just see you tugging on a net of haddock. The fish would probably yank you right into the drink."

So I began to work out a lot and eat second helpings at dinner. Soon I could almost beat Dad at arm wrestling. And I went on waiting.

I live in Gloucester, on the coast of Massachusetts. It would be hard to grow up in this area and *not* love fishing and the sea. Even Mom, before she died, liked to go out on the *Sea Angel* on weekends. My brother, Tommy, had been fishing with Dad ever since he graduated from college.

By the time I turned sixteen, Tommy had moved down to Boston to go to law school. Dad said that he understood. But after that, I'd often catch a lonely look on Dad's face. Each morning, he would take the *Sea Angel* out by himself.

One night, after dinner, I asked Dad a third time to take me fishing with him.

"What about school?" he asked.

"I can fish with you every weekend until school lets out," I told him. "During the summer, we can fish every day."

Dad seemed to be searching for reasons to turn me down. Suddenly, I got angry. "You've taught me a lot about the sea. But you never let me help out when it really counts. What's wrong? Do you think I can't do the work?"

Dad looked at me with hard, steady eyes. It was the sort of going-over I'd seen him give a boat. He wanted to know how strong, how seaworthy I would be. Finally, he took my hand in his and gave it a tight squeeze. "OK, Terry, you've just become the whole crew of the *Sea Angel.*"

Late in July, we went out overnight to fish for tuna. We worked very hard the first day.

When I woke up the next morning, the first thing I smelled was eggs and ham. I could hear Dad cooking in the galley. I had slept too long, and the sky outside my window was bright and clear.

I was just pulling on my boots when the first crash shook the boat. It felt as if a giant fist of water had slammed into us. The *Sea Angel* rolled from side to side like a toy boat in a bathtub. I heard the pans and plates go flying about the galley. In a moment, Dad came running through the cabin. He grabbed his coat and climbed up on deck.

"What was it, Dad? Did we hit something?"

Dad didn't answer at first. He was leaning from the bow, looking back and forth. I couldn't see anything nearby that could have run into us. Dad was looking hard at the dark water.

Then I saw it—a giant black fin that broke through the waves. It was moving toward the boat from the port side.

"Hey, Dad! Over here!" I shouted. "It's way too big for a shark's fin," I said. "Could it be a dolphin?"

He shook his head. "Too big for that, too. Look!"

We saw four or five more of the dark fins knifing through the water, circling close to the *Sea Angel*.

"Orcas!" Dad shouted. "Wait here, Terry!" Then he went below deck, leaving me alone.

So it was a pack of orcas — *killer whales*. Just saying their name made me feel icy cold inside. Dad once told me that people call them killers, but they really eat only squid and other fish. He said they may look fierce, but they have never been known to kill humans. "That doesn't mean there won't be a first time," I thought.

Now I could see the great black body of the lead killer whale. It dipped in and out of the waves. It looked as long as a school bus.

Dad came on deck with two life jackets and handed one to me. But I couldn't take my eyes off the killer whales. The leader had just dived deep. I watched the huge tail disappear below the water.

"What's going to happen?" I asked as I watched Dad inflate the life raft.

"Probably nothing, honey," he said, giving me a quick smile. "I called the Coast Guard on the radio just in case . . ."

But before Dad could finish his sentence, something like an explosion ripped through the heart of the *Sea Angel*. The force of the blow threw me into the cold water. I can still hear the awful sound of wood splintering as the killer whale hit the bow.

Before I knew what had happened, I was treading water. I looked all around, but Dad was nowhere in sight. I watched helplessly as the *Sea Angel* broke up and sank. I was too shocked to cry.

The bright yellow life raft drifted up to me. I tried to pull myself up on top of it. Again and again, I lost my grip and slipped back into the water. Then, one more try, and I was lying inside the raft, gasping for breath. When I could get enough air, I began to scream as loud as I could. "Dad! Where are you?"

Then I saw him. He was bobbing in the waves about thirty feet away. His life jacket was holding him up, but he wasn't answering me. What should I do? Could I swim to him? Would I have the strength to tow him back to the raft?

I had to do something. I was about to jump back into the water when I saw the tall black fin breaking the surface. One of the killer whales was swimming toward Dad. I remember wanting to scream. But when I opened my mouth, no sound came out.

The killer whale was close to Dad now. I wanted to close my eyes, but I just couldn't. I saw Dad bounce out of the waves. The killer whale turned and came at him again.

I couldn't put it all together at first. I just stared dumbly. Then it came to me. The killer whale wasn't attacking Dad. It was bumping him, nosing him up out of the water. The whale looked just like a trained seal playing with a beach ball.

After three passes, the orca dived, leaving Dad floating near me. He was close enough for me to grab hold of his jacket. I struggled but finally got him into the raft. I looked around. The killer whales were gone, and we were alone.

I'll never forget that day. Dad probably won't, either—what he remembers of it. After we were safe, he kept saying over and over again how proud he was of me. He couldn't quite believe the part about the killer whale bouncing him around. He said what mattered was that I could stand up under stress. I had done as well as any crew member he had ever known.

Dad decided then that he could depend on me. I'm now Dad's new partner. And I'm part owner of the *Sea Angel II.*

FOLLOW-UP

1. What happened to the *Sea Angel?*

2. At the end of the story, why was Terry's dad proud of her?

3. Do you think that Terry might decide to make a living by fishing? Why do you think that?

Killer Whales

They have been called killers and wolves of the sea. People have feared them for ages. They were believed to attack almost anything — even people!

Not long ago, scientists began studying orcas, or killer whales. They still don't know much about these animals. But they do know this: Captive orcas are gentle and playful. And, as far as we know, wild orcas have never killed a human being, even when they could have. In the 1970's, for example, orcas wrecked a boat off the California coast. The crew had been cruelly teasing the animals. The orcas could have attacked the men. Instead, they let the men swim to shore unharmed.

So what is the truth about killer whales?

Killers and Whales

Orcas are really more closely related to dolphins than to the biggest whales. Unlike the big whales, orcas have huge teeth. Those teeth can be frightening to look at! Killers are also big, though not as big as the large whales. Killers may grow up to thirty feet long and weigh seven tons. And that big fin on a killer's back may even be taller than you are!

Killers as Hunters

A killer's diet includes seals, fish, water birds, squid, dolphins, and even large whales. They are called wolves of the sea because of the way they hunt.

A pod of killer whales comes to the surface to rest.

Like wolves, orcas often use teamwork. They may trap their victims by forming a circle around them. Each orca then takes a turn darting in and out to feed. Orcas may even smash thick slabs of ice to pieces to reach a seal. No place is safe from orcas!

Killers' Family Life

Killers live in groups called pods. There may be up to fifty killers in a pod. Some scientists believe that these killer-whale families stay together for life.

The killers in a pod look out for one another. They will help a mother take care of a newborn killer calf. And they will protect a hurt or sick killer in the pod.

Pod members can keep in touch, even if they become separated from one another. Like dolphins, killers make clicking and whistling sounds. These sounds can travel at least *three miles* underwater!

Where Killers Live

Killer whales prefer colder waters, like those near Antarctica or off the western Canadian coast. But that doesn't mean you won't see a tall black fin off the Atlantic coast. Killers have been seen in every ocean of the world.

A female killer whale swims with her calf.

There's nothing to getting a date
for the big dance.
Or is there?

The Dance

by Ellen Rabinowich

All my best buddies were going to the dance. Pete, Joe, and even Bob the Animal had all found someone who said yes.

"So who are you taking?" Pete asked me after swim practice on Tuesday.

"It's still a surprise," I said.

"I'll be surprised, all right," Pete said. "If you take anyone. Nothing personal, Mark."

"What are you talking about?"

"The dance is only three days away. And I bet you still don't have a date."

"No sweat," I told him. "I've got it all locked up." But that was a lie. I had already asked Jill Roth to the dance. She had said sorry, but she was going with someone else. A total waste.

I remember how I felt afterward — pretty bad. I liked Jill. She was a good swimmer and she knew how to joke around. I always thought we hit it off pretty well. I was kind of surprised when she said no.

"So you were shot down," I told myself. Big deal. I could always ask someone else.

But I couldn't. I know it sounds crazy. After all, I'd been afraid of things before. I remember my first time on the high dive. Sure, I was scared. But I fought it and dived right off. Then there was Frank, the school big shot. Sure, he scared me. But I managed to tell him off once. But this time I'd lost my nerve. I was afraid of one simple word—*no.*

Usually I fall asleep in five minutes flat. That night I tossed and turned. I couldn't stop thinking about the dance. Of course, I could go stag. Lots of guys do that. But I had told everyone that I had a date. How would it look if I walked in alone? I was beginning to think that a tornado was the best thing that could happen. Then they'd cancel the dance. "Fat chance," I admitted to myself.

Finally, I decided to make a list. I found paper and a pencil. I put down the names of three girls I might want to ask—Janet, Pam, and Maxine. Then I did something else. I listed the odds. I wanted to know what the chances were of each of them saying yes.

Janet was great-looking, a real teen-model type, and she always said "Hi" to everyone. But Janet had a boyfriend. Scratch that one.

Pam was easy to talk to. She never made people feel as if they had said the wrong thing. But Pam was very popular. I put her down as a long shot, ten to one.

Then there was Maxine. Maxine was a natural comic. She always made our class crack up. But I hardly knew her, so I put her down as eight to one.

I looked over my list. Boy, did I hate doing this. I was ready to chuck the whole thing, to forget it and stay home. But I wanted to go. Besides, if I didn't show, people might think that every girl I'd asked had said no.

So, I made another list. This one was more practical. I listed the three girls most likely to say yes.

Nancy was a real showoff. I think most guys were afraid of her. Actually, I wasn't even sure I wanted to be with her. But she was better than nothing, so I put her down as three to one.

Betty was a real baby. She liked to pretend that she couldn't do anything. But some guys like that kind of girl. I put her down as four to one.

Then there was Sue. She seemed smart and nice, but she was so shy that she never talked to anyone. Then again, you can't always tell with shy girls. Sometimes they're secretly in love with someone. I put her down as five to one.

Then I looked over my list. It was plain that the safest bet was Nancy, the showoff.

The next day I went to school, feeling much better. I decided to tackle the second list. That way, I had three pretty good chances. Why should I sweat it? I decided to ask Nancy first. After all, she was my safest bet.

"Hey, Nancy," I said when I saw her in the hall. "What are you doing Friday night?"

"You mean the night of the dance?"

"That's right."

Nancy gave me a funny look. "Why?" she asked.

"Well, I . . . well, I . . . " I could feel my mouth go dry and my hands get damp. I couldn't get the words out. "Well," I finally said, "I'm going, and I was hoping I'd see you there."

"Oh, you'll see me," Nancy said. "I'm going with Tim, and we're going to dance every dance."

"You blew it," I said to myself as Nancy walked away. But then, that was OK. Nancy wouldn't have gone with me anyway.

Next, I tried Betty. Now that I had a little practice, it had to be easier.

"Hi, Betty," I said when I saw her during lunch. "Got your dancing shoes ready for Friday night?"

"I can't dance," she said.

"Oh. Does that mean you don't want to go?"

"Why?" she asked.

"Well, I . . . well, I . . . " I was stuck. I just couldn't ask her. What if she said no? "Well, I was hoping I'd see you there," I said weakly.

"You will." Betty smiled. "I'm going with Rob. He can't dance, either."

Now I had only one shot left — shy Sue. The more I thought about it, the more nervous I got. I liked Sue. Even though she was shy, there was something about her that told me she had a lot going for her. I just *had* to make myself ask her.

"Hi, Sue," I said when I saw her after class. "Ready for Friday night?"

"Friday?"

"The night of the dance."

Sue looked down. "Why do you ask?"

"Well, I . . . well, I . . . " I couldn't blow this one. It was my last chance. "Well, I was wondering if you were going," I blurted out.

There. I had asked her. Or at least I thought I had.

"I did want to go," Sue said. "I asked Jules Wilson, but he said no."

I was stunned. "You asked him?"

"Yes. I've always liked him. But I guess I was too shy to show it."

I took a deep breath. "Sue —"

"Yes?"

"Would you like to go to the dance with me?"

Sue smiled. "Yes," she said. "Yes, I would."

Suddenly, I felt ten feet tall. Why was I so worried? Asking girls out — there's nothing to it!

FOLLOW-UP

1. Mark tried to get a date for the dance four times. What happened each time?

2. How are Sue and Mark alike?

3. Will it be easier now for Mark to ask a girl out? Why do you think that?

What makes a good athlete — skill or luck?
Some athletes aren't taking any chances.

With Any Kind of Luck by Kathlyn Gay

Athletes know that it takes hard work and skill to win in sports. But a little bit of luck might help, too! So, many players — and coaches and fans — try to bring good luck or chase away bad luck in different ways. It's a little like wishing on a star. You might not believe in magic, but you hope your dreams or wishes will come true anyway.

One down-on-his-luck story is often told about a great baseball player of the past. Dizzy Dean was a pitcher for the St. Louis Cardinals. He always carried a rabbit's foot with him. Once he left his lucky charm in the pocket of a suit that he sent to the cleaner. He forgot where the charm was. When his team lost the next game, Dizzy thought that he had brought them bad luck. The Cardinals didn't win another game until Dizzy found his rabbit's foot.

Runners, racing car drivers, bowlers, football players — many people in sports — carry charms. Sometimes the good-luck piece is a coin or a smooth stone. Or it might be a stuffed animal or a medal on a chain. Even dirty old socks sometimes are thought to be lucky.

In team sports, many players like to wear a special number for luck. Some wear the number 13, which is supposed to bring bad luck. But players like it because they think they can change 13 to a lucky number.

Do you know why many baseball players never step on the foul line when running onto or off the field? "Stepping on the line brings bad luck," as the saying goes. Do you know why some tennis players like to bounce the ball seven times before serving it? That's for good luck, too.

There are about as many good-luck rituals in sports as there are people who play, coach, or just watch. For one thing, many players like to put their uniforms on in the same way. Maybe the left sock always goes on first and the shirt always goes on last. Some athletes always eat the same food before competing. Any change might bring bad luck, they say.

Some people go to great trouble to ward off bad luck. For many years, an Ohio high-school basketball team took part in the same ritual before every game. The coach told his five starting players to lie face down in a circle on the floor. He asked the players to touch hands in the middle of the circle. Then the coach went around to give each player a good-luck pat on the back. The team won 76 games in a row.

For three years, that same coach wore the same suit during every game. In fact, he wore the seat of the pants thin from slipping and sliding on the bench. The coach had to keep having his pants fixed so that he could wear the same suit, game after game. All for good luck, of course!

Sports fans also like to wear lucky clothes. Many fans have special hats or sweaters that they wear to games. If a team has a lucky color, then the fans, coaches, and players may wear that color. In one school, purple was the color — purple socks, purple shoelaces, purple towels. Purple was everywhere for luck.

Maybe you use magic in sports, too. Do you cross your fingers for your team? Do you shake or slap hands with teammates for luck before playing a game? Do you have a lucky number, or put a lucky coin in your shoe? Do you repeat a saying to bring you luck?

If your kind of magic doesn't work, don't give up. After all, you might see the first star in the sky tonight. You can always wish on it — unless a dark cloud passes over the moon, or a black cat crosses your path, or . . .

Oh, well, you may not win every game. But with any kind of luck, you could win a few!

READING LABELS

Every day, we use things from bottles, boxes, and cans. All of those containers have labels on them. We should read those labels carefully. Even when we think we know how to use a product, we could be wrong. Every year, people die because they use products in the wrong way. How can labels help you use a product in the right way?

Read the *whole* label on a product *before* you use it. You will get better results and protect yourself, too. A label will usually tell you three important things. First, it tells you what the product can and can't do. Second, it tells you how the product may be harmful and what to do to protect yourself. Third, it tells you how to use the product.

Make the Right Choice

Valerie and June decided to earn money one summer. They hired themselves out to do household chores. They bought cleaners, rubber gloves, brushes, paper towels, and two pails. Their first job was to clean a kitchen and bathroom.

Valerie decided to do the kitchen floor first. "Sure is greasy," she said. "Hey, June, pass me the oven cleaner."

"What for?"

"There's greasy stuff on the floor," said Valerie.

June looked up. "You trying to get us fired?" she shouted. "You can't use that stuff on the floor!"

"Sure you can," said Valerie. "It says on the can that it takes off baked-on grease."

"That means inside the oven. That stuff will eat through the floor to the basement! Read the label."

In the very first part of the label, Valerie read these words: BEFORE USING THIS PRODUCT, PRO-TECT THE FLOOR WITH NEWSPAPER.

It was a good thing that June had read the label. Oven cleaner was not the right choice for cleaning the floor!

Before you choose any product, think about what you want it to do. Then read the labels of several products. Choose the product that is best for that job.

Shown below is part of a label from an ammonia bottle. What can you use ammonia for? Find out by reading the sections called SMALL JOBS, GENERAL CLEANING, and TOUGH JOBS. What kinds of small cleaning jobs can you use ammonia for? What big cleaning jobs is it good for? What tough cleaning jobs is it good for? Notice that you *cannot* use ammonia to clean aluminum pans.

Once you have chosen the right product for a job, you must make sure you know how to use it safely.

CARTER'S AMMONIA

Carter's ammonia is great for all of your household cleaning chores. It cleans the kitchen, bathroom, just about anywhere in your house.

SMALL JOBS: Mix Carter's ammonia in a spray bottle (4–8 tablespoons with warm water) to clean up sinks and counters.

GENERAL CLEANING: Mix ½ cup of Carter's ammonia per gallon of warm water to clean floors, tiles, walls, woodwork—any large area.

TOUGH JOBS: Use Carter's ammonia full strength to remove scuff marks and grease. Pour Carter's in your drains to keep them clean and fresh.

DO NOT USE TO SOAK ALUMINUM PANS.

Study the Warnings

Valerie's next task was spraying for bugs. She opened the door where the snack foods were. She took the cap off the insect spray. June looked up.

"Hey, did you clean out those shelves first?"

"Don't need to. They're not dirty," said Valerie.

"That's not what I meant," groaned June. "You can't spray that stuff anywhere near food."

"Oh," said Valerie. She looked at the label. Sure enough, under the word *warning* were these words: DO NOT SPRAY NEAR FOOD.

Labels often tell you in what ways a product may be harmful. They also will give directions for first-aid treatment. *Always* read this part of the label, even before you read the directions for using the product.

You can spot the warnings on a label by looking for any of these words: *caution, danger,* or *warning.* Which of these words is on the part of the ammonia label shown on page 69?

Read the warning on the label. It lists some things that you should not do. For one thing, you don't want to get ammonia in your eyes. So don't rub your eyes with a hand that's been in ammonia! Also, ammonia is a very strong cleaner. You don't want to keep your hands in it for very long. If a cleaning job will take a while, what should you wear on your hands? Rubber gloves would be a good choice.

CAUTION: Avoid contact with eyes and prolonged contact with skin. Do not swallow. Avoid breathing fumes. Use in a well-ventilated area.

Treatments:

EXTERNAL: Skin—Flood with water. Eyes— Flush with water and get medical treatment.

INTERNAL: Give milk or water immediately. Call physician immediately.

DO NOT MIX WITH BLEACH OR OTHER HOUSEHOLD CLEANERS.

The label also tells you not to swallow ammonia or breathe the fumes. It says that you should use ammonia only in a *well-ventilated area*. That means that you should always leave doors and windows open where you are working. The fumes can then escape. You should open doors and windows when you use many other household cleaners, too.

The warning on a label is always followed by directions for first-aid treatment. Often you will see the words *external* and *internal*.

External means "outside." If you get the product in your eyes or on your skin, you should follow those directions. What should you do if you get ammonia in your eyes?

Internal means "inside." You take something internally by swallowing it. The word *immediately* means "right away." What should you give immediately to a person who has swallowed ammonia? The directions also tell you to call a physician, or doctor, immediately. You should call a doctor when *any* household cleaner has been swallowed.

What is the last warning on the label? Right. *Never* mix ammonia with bleach or any other household cleaner. The result could be a deadly gas.

Once you have read all the warnings, you are ready to follow the directions for using the product.

Read the Directions

By this time, Valerie decided it might be safer to clean the bathroom. Wrong! She took such a long time to clean out the tub drain that June went in to check on things.

"Now what's up?" June asked.

"This drain is really plugged. I need to pour some more of this drain stuff down — a third time."

By now, June knew what to expect. "Did you read the directions?" she asked.

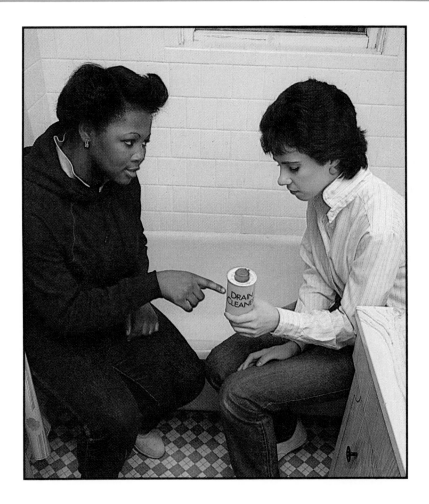

"Yeah, most of them," said Valerie.

"Valerie, you have to read through *all* of the directions. The last step says you shouldn't use the stuff more than *twice*. . . . Val?"

"What?"

"Take out the trash. That's a safe job."

The directions tell you how to use a product. Before starting the job, read *all* of the directions to get the whole picture.

Read the first part of the ammonia label again. How much ammonia and water should you use to clean a kitchen floor? How much ammonia should you use to remove grease? When you are ready to use the ammonia, double-check the directions. Once you've done that, you know you can use the ammonia safely and get good results.

Remember to read labels whenever you use any product. Read labels on paint, glue, first-aid cream, mouthwash — everything. First, read to find out what the product can be used for. Second, be sure you read the warning and first-aid directions. And third, read through the directions to find out how to use the product.

Reading labels might save you time. It might also save your life.

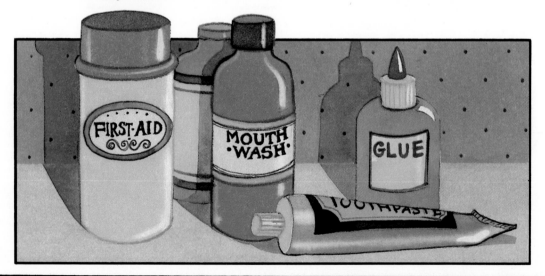

Questions

Use the ammonia label on pages 67 and 69 to answer these questions.

1. How would you use ammonia to get scuff marks off a kitchen floor?

2. If you have a small cut on your finger and you get ammonia in it, what should you do?

3. Why would ammonia *not* be the best cleaner to use in a long, narrow hallway?

Carly didn't know that she was about to take the ride of her life!

THE RIDE

I found an empty bench on the boardwalk and sat down to wait for Alma. I could hear the waves crashing on the beach behind me. Ahead of me was the Rocky Neck Amusement Park. I watched the bright blue, yellow, and green lights dance in the night sky. I listened to the sounds of the park — the merry-go-round music and the cries from the people on the roller coaster. Everything blended together.

"Hey, Carlota! Carly! Wake up!" It was Alma.

"I must have been daydreaming," I muttered.

"It's a little late for daydreaming," said Alma. She sat down beside me and passed me a bucket of popcorn.

"No, thanks," I said. "What time is it?"

Alma held her watch up to the light. "It's almost ten," she answered and reached for more popcorn.

"Good," I said. "There's just enough time for one more ride. I still have two tickets left. Let's finish off with a spin on The Tornado."

Alma rolled her eyes. "You spin and I'll sit," she answered. "Listen, Carly. I don't like that ride. All it does is go around and around and around." She closed her eyes. "I get sick just thinking about it."

"OK, Alma," I said. I didn't want to be unreasonable. "Finish your popcorn. I'll meet you back here after the ride."

Alma waved at me. Well, it wasn't much of a wave. Her hand was full of popcorn.

There was a long line for The Tornado. There always is. As I stood in line, I could feel the excitement building around me. The Tornado does that to people.

The line moved pretty fast. I handed one of my tickets to the attendant. I put the other one in my pocket. I climbed into the car and buckled myself in. Then I took a deep breath, braced my hands against the guardrail, and got ready.

The car leaped forward. The Tornado had begun.

It gained speed. Around and around we went —
up a big spiral. I looked out. The lights of the amusement park spun around and around until they were a
big blur. The sounds of the park seemed to knock
into one another.

Suddenly, everything was still. We were perched
like climbers at the peak of a mountain. Then The
Tornado shifted gears. We started going around and
around again — backward — down the spiral. We
picked up speed, and once again everything was a
blur. Faster and faster — and faster.

Something was wrong. I had been on the ride enough times to know that. We were going *too* fast. The top half of my body was pressed forward. No matter how hard I tried, I couldn't sit up.

The screeching and clatter of the cars grew louder and louder. The racket was deafening. I wanted to cry out, but I couldn't get my breath. Faster and faster. The back of my head felt as if it were going to explode. That was when I blacked out.

"Hey, Carlota! Carly! Wake up!"

My eyes popped open. Alma was standing in front of me.

"I must have been daydreaming," I muttered. I stretched and rubbed the back of my head.

"It's a little late for daydreaming," said Alma. She sat down beside me and passed me a bucket of popcorn.

"No, thanks," I said. I was thinking about my ride on The Tornado. What a ride! I was also wondering how I had gotten back to this bench. I must really have been in a daze. I looked over at Alma. When I had left her the first time, she was finishing off a bucket of popcorn. Now, here she was, starting on her second bucket. Alma eats enough for two people but never gains an ounce.

"Alma," I said, a little annoyed. "How can you put away *two* buckets of popcorn?"

She looked puzzled. "Two buckets? What are you talking about? I've got only one bucket. See?"

I shook my head. "That's not what I meant, but it doesn't matter. Come on, I'm tired. Let's go home."

Alma stopped chewing. "Go home? Now?" she asked. "Well, that's a first! You always go for a ride on The Tornado before you go home."

I turned and stared at her. "Are you crazy!" I yelped. "I just went for a ride on The Tornado. In fact, I think it was my *last* ride on The Tornado!"

Alma rolled her eyes. "Who are you kidding?" she asked. "I've been with you all night — up until five minutes ago." She laughed and grabbed another fistful of popcorn. "You're such a kidder," she said.

My stomach was doing flip-flops. "What's going on here?" I asked myself. Did I just dream I went for a ride on The Tornado?

There was one way to find out. I reached down into the pocket of my jeans. If I still had two tickets, then the whole thing was a dream. My hand closed on some paper. I pulled it out and looked. I was holding one ticket. Now I was certain.

I grabbed the side of the bench to steady myself. I thought about what had happened on that ride. I had gone backward at high speed — *very* high speed.

"Alma?" I asked, trying to keep my voice from sounding strange. "What time is it?"

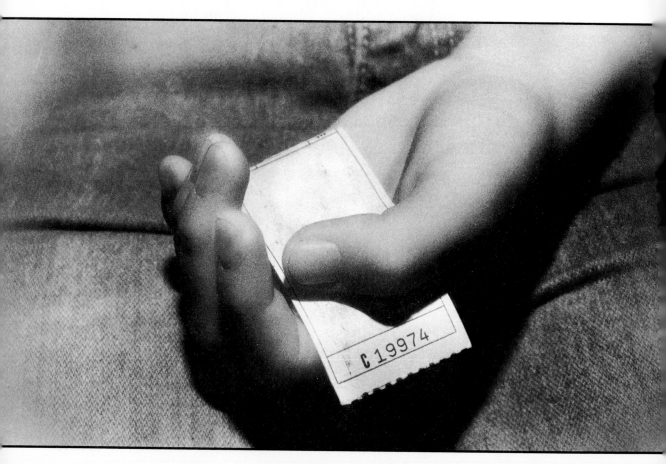

Alma held her watch up to the light. "It's almost ten," she answered.

Almost ten. I was back where I had started — *before* I went for a ride on The Tornado. What would happen if I went on the ride now? Would the same thing happen all over again? Would the machine break down again and send me back to where I had started — again?

I had to find out. I just had to.

"OK, Alma," I said. "Finish your popcorn. I'll meet you back here after the ride."

Alma waved at me. Her hand was full of popcorn.

FOLLOW-UP

1. What was so unusual about the ride that Carly took on The Tornado?

2. After her ride on The Tornado, Carly slowly began to understand that something was wrong. What odd things did she notice? Tell about them in the order that Carly noticed them.

The History of Roller Coasters

by Barbara Seuling

Past

The Switchback Railway opened about one hundred years ago at the Coney Island amusement park in New York. It was the first American railroad built just for fun. People in its railroad car coasted a few hundred feet. Then, at the end of the line, workers turned the car around. They pushed it over a switch and up a hill. At the top, the force of gravity did the rest. The car then coasted back along another track.

The Switchback Railway was the work of La-Marcus Thompson. He had seen people paying to ride in coal cars in an old coal mine. Why not try the same thing at an amusement park? Because he did just that, Thompson is given credit for building the first roller coaster in the United States.

The Switchback Railway on Coney Island

Since Thompson's time, people have been making his design better. First, a machine was built to replace the workers who pushed the car. Each coaster car was attached by gears to a chain under the tracks. The machine then pulled the car uphill. Later on, taller coasters with extra dips, twists, and turns were built. By the 1930's, the first loop was added to the tracks. Cars zoomed down a steep hill into the loop.

The Big Dipper on Coney Island, about 1930

The speed of the cars created enough force to hold the upside-down riders safely in their seats. The loop helped make roller coasters one of the most popular rides of all time.

Present

Roller coasters today are bigger, faster, and better than ever. Computers check their speed and safety. The new rails are made of steel tubes. They replaced the old, flat, metal tracks. Nylon wheels have replaced the old metal wheels on the cars. The curves of the tracks are banked, or tilted, so that the cars

can make smooth turns at top speeds. All of these changes have helped make a faster, smoother ride.

People still love the roller coaster. The newer coasters have been given names like The Corkscrew and The Great American Scream Machine. One of the biggest and fastest roller coasters is The American Eagle in Gurnee, Illinois. Built in 1981, it climbs 12 stories high. Then it plummets 147 feet into an underground tunnel at a speed of more than 60 miles per hour.

The Corkscrew at Cedar Point in Sandusky, Ohio

Other modern coasters have dazzling double and triple loops. Some swoop down through fog or total darkness. In Sandusky, Ohio, there is a park with six roller coasters. No wonder Sandusky has been called the roller coaster capital of the world!

LaMarcus Thompson's simple roller coaster must have been exciting in the 1880's. But the modern roller coasters would make that ride look very tame. The roller coaster has grown up since then. It has become a ride of the Space Age.

Hans Muller was a set designer for a TV program. He was good — *too* good.

Security Check

Adapted from a story by Arthur C. Clarke

Hans Muller was by nature a simple man with simple needs. He worked with his hands, and he took pride in everything he did. His workshop, where he made and repaired wood and metal objects, was a large room in a deserted warehouse. Most of the building was already boarded up. Soon the structure would be torn down, and Hans would have to move.

Hans had always managed to make just enough money to get by. But now, he felt the need for more. An idea came to him one night while he was watching television.

Now, Hans had never cared much for television. Most programs were a waste of his time. But recently, a show had come on the air that captured his interest. He watched it every week. It was about a strange and thrilling world of battling spaceships, distant planets, and odd creatures. It was the world of Captain Zipp, Commander of the Space Fleet.

It was many weeks before Hans's enjoyment of the show wore off. The first thing that began to annoy him was the furniture in Captain Zipp's future world. Hans could not believe that the furniture of the future would be in such bad taste.

He also thought very little of the weapons that Captain Zipp used. It was true that Hans did not pretend to understand how a proton disintegrator gun might work. Still, he felt there was no reason why it should look *that* clumsy. Nothing inside the spaceship — not even the clothes worn by the actors — was convincing.

Now Hans had an idea. He had heard that there was money in TV. So, being a clever man, he sat down and began to draw. He brought his ideas to the producer of the show. It did not take much to convince the producer that Hans's designs were special.

Already, some of Captain Zipp's most loyal fans had begun to tire of the old set designs. And here were designs of props and costumes that looked *so* real. There was nothing phony about them.

Hans was hired on the spot. He asked only to be left alone in his workshop. All that he wanted to do was to design the sets and props. They could be made somewhere else. Hans was an artist, not a factory.

Within six months, Captain Zipp had been completely changed. The show had become a great success. To all the Captain Zipp fans, it was not just a show about the future—it *was* the future. Even the actors found themselves believing that they lived in the year 2100. Life in the present sometimes annoyed them because they no longer had the gadgets that made their lives so easy on the set.

But Hans knew nothing of this. He refused to see anyone but the producer, and he did all his business over the telephone. He watched the show each week to make sure that his ideas had been carried out faithfully.

One Sunday night, he was working late, putting the final touches to a space helmet. Suddenly, he felt that he was no longer alone. Slowly he turned from the workbench and faced the door. There were two men standing beside it. The door had been locked. How could it have been opened so quietly? The men did not move as they watched him. Hans felt his heart begin to beat faster. Robbers!

"Who are you? What are you doing here?" Hans asked.

One of the men moved toward him, while the other remained watching from the door. They were both wearing new overcoats, with hats low down on their heads. Hans could not see their faces. They were too well dressed to be common robbers.

"There's no need to be alarmed, Mr. Muller," said the nearer man, as if he were reading Hans's very thoughts. "This isn't a holdup. We're from— Security."

"I don't understand," said Hans.

The man by the door reached into his coat and pulled out a pile of photographs. He looked through them until he found the ones he wanted. He passed them to the man standing near Hans.

"You've given us quite a headache, Mr. Muller," said the man who had spoken before. "It's taken us two weeks to find you. Your boss refused to tell us much. However, here we are, and I'd like you to answer some questions."

"I'm not a spy!" Hans said as he began to understand what was going on. "You can't do this. I'm a loyal American."

The man ignored the outburst. He handed over a photograph. "Do you know what this is?" he asked.

"Yes," replied Hans. "It's the inside of Captain Zipp's spaceship."

"And you designed it?" asked the man.

"Yes," said Hans.

The man handed over another photograph. "And what about this?" he asked.

"That's the Antarean city of Paldar, as seen from the air," said Hans.

"Your own idea?" asked the man.

"Certainly," Hans replied.

"And this?"

"Oh, the proton gun," said Hans quickly. "I was quite proud of that."

"Tell me, Mr. Muller — are these all your own ideas?"

"Yes," said Hans, annoyed. "*I* don't steal from other people."

His questioner turned to the man by the door and spoke for a few minutes in a voice too low for Hans to hear. They seemed to reach agreement on some point. They both turned back to Hans before he could make his planned grab for the telephone.

"I'm sorry," said the man. "But there has been a security leak. It may be purely by chance, but that does not change the problem. We will have to question you further. Please come with us."

There was such power in the stranger's voice that Hans said nothing and reached for his coat. Somehow, he no longer questioned that these men were from Security. He never thought of asking for proof of who they were.

He was worried but not yet alarmed. Of course, it was clear what had happened. He remembered hearing about a science-fiction writer during World War II who had unknowingly revealed the secret of the atom bomb. When so much secret work was going on, such things were likely to happen. Hans wondered just what it was that he had given away.

At the doorway, he looked back into his workshop and at the men who were following him.

"It's all a silly mistake," said Hans. "If I *did* show anything secret in the program, it was just by chance. I've never done anything to annoy the FBI."

It was then that the second man spoke for the first time. He spoke in very bad English and with a very strange accent. "What is the FBI?" he asked.

But Hans didn't hear him. He had just seen the spaceship.

FOLLOW-UP

1. What made Hans decide to start drawing designs for the Captain Zipp show?

2. Where do you think the two men were from?

3. Why did the two men want Hans?

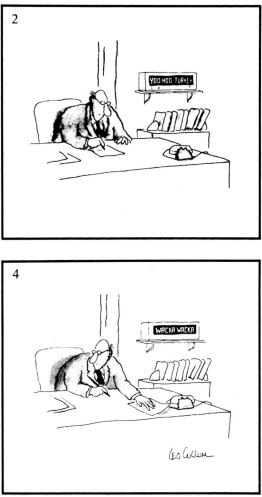

Reprinted with permission from The
Saturday Evening Post Company, © 1980.

Is a mean mugger any match for Kay's dog, Wolf?

Wolf Captures Ski Mask

by Irene Elmer

I met Kay walking Wolf the other day. "Hi, there, Wolf," I said. I make it a point to be polite to big dogs.

Wolf wagged his tail. I took that as a good sign.

"He knows that you and I are friends," said Kay. "He's so smart. He just seems to know what people are thinking."

Wolf stood up on his hind legs and put his front paws on my shoulders. Standing up, Wolf is as tall as I am. He's coal black and weighs maybe 75 pounds. No lie — he's *huge*.

"Good thing he's friendly," I said as Wolf licked my face.

"Down," said Kay. "Sit." Wolf took his paws off my shoulders. He sat beside Kay and followed me with his eyes.

"He's friendly because you're my friend," said Kay. "If someone tried to hurt me, Wolf wouldn't be so friendly."

Wolf kept on watching me. "I bet," I said.

"It's because he's a Belgian sheepdog," said Kay. "Belgians can sense how people feel. They can just tell somehow when something is wrong. That's why they make ideal police dogs."

I stepped back a little. Wolf didn't miss a move.

"And they notice everything," said Kay.

Wolf decided I was OK after all. He lay down on Kay's foot.

"He's so smart," said Kay. "Of course, he's young. Once in a while, he makes a little mistake."

"Um . . . what kind of mistake?" I asked, looking uneasily at Wolf. Even a little mistake could cost you an arm or leg, I was sure.

Kay thought a moment. Then she started to laugh. "Well," she said, "do you remember Ski Mask?"

Of course I remembered Ski Mask. Everyone in our neighborhood remembered Ski Mask. Ski Mask was a mugger, and he was *mean*. I won't even tell you what he did. He was called Ski Mask because that's what he wore. That was so no one could tell who he was, I guess.

Ski Mask is in jail now, where he belongs. I hope he stays there. But before he was caught, people were pretty scared. We were all afraid to go out alone at night. We even set up neighborhood patrols. The police helped us. I never did hear how they finally caught him.

"Don't tell me it was Wolf that caught Ski Mask!" I said. Kay just laughed.

"Shall we tell her, Wolf?" she said. Wolf looked up at Kay and seemed to grin. His tail swept back and forth on the sidewalk.

"Remember?" said Kay. "Ski Mask worked at night. He picked on people who were out alone, so patrols were set up.

"My mom was on one patrol. She said it was really scary. The people on the patrol were really tense. But they figured that as long as the patrol was out, Ski Mask wouldn't dare show up. If he did show up, they'd get him. There was a big reward for catching him. Remember?"

Kay stopped. She could see that I wanted her to go on. Kay likes to make a story sound exciting.

"Well," she said slowly, "one night Wolf kept bothering me to go out. He was restless because he'd been shut in all day. I got his leash and told my mom that I was going to take him for a walk.

"Mom wasn't worried about me going out. She knew I'd be safe if Wolf was with me. And besides, the patrol was out. There were always three people on the patrol. That night it was Mr. Wells and Mr. Alvarez and Mrs. Fracatelli.

"I wasn't scared — I was excited. I'd been thinking about that reward of ten thousand dollars. I know it was dumb, but I had this crazy idea — what if Wolf and I could somehow catch Ski Mask? I had already planned how I would spend the money. I was going to buy a stereo for me and a car for Mom. And a big steak for Wolf.

"Anyway, I put the leash on Wolf and we went out. It was around 9:00. It was real dark. The only light was right under the street lights—that cold, green light, you know? It was very quiet—so quiet that it was spooky. No one else was out on the street. Now, I don't know if I can explain this. But even though there was nobody out, the whole neighborhood felt tense. The *air* felt tense.

"Wolf sensed it right away. He was alert. He pricked up his ears, and he kept pulling on the leash and growling a little. You could just tell he sensed that something wasn't quite right.

"I was starting to get a little scared. I began to think that maybe I shouldn't have come out. Ski Mask could be anywhere—maybe right behind me!

"But I didn't panic. I just told myself that if Ski Mask was behind me, too bad for him. Wolf would know if he was there, even if I didn't.

"Well, we got to the corner of Elm Street. You know, that corner where the trees grow out over the sidewalk? The street light on that corner was out, so it was really dark. I should have avoided that corner, but something made me go on.

"It was *deathly* quiet. It was so quiet, I could hear Wolf's nails clicking on the sidewalk. Suddenly, Wolf bolted. He just jerked the leash right out of my hand. I was stunned. He had never, ever done that before. Wolf is very strong, and he nearly knocked me down. For a minute, I couldn't tell which way he'd gone.

"And then, halfway up Elm Street, I heard the most awful racket — barking and snarling. It sounded worse than any dogfight I had ever heard.

"I ran up Elm Street. I was excited. Of course, I was thinking about the reward." Kay stopped again. She looked at me and smiled.

"Go on," I said.

"You want me to go on?"

"Sure."

"You want to know who Wolf had caught?" she asked.

Sometimes Kay drives me nuts. "Nope," I told her. "I bet he hadn't caught anybody. I bet old Wolf was just chasing a cat."

"Oh, he'd caught somebody, all right," said Kay. "Three people. Wolf had backed them up against a wall — Mr. Wells and Mr. Alvarez and Mrs. Fracatelli. Poor Wolf. He was so excited. He had captured the patrol." Kay laughed. "So that's how Wolf caught Ski Mask — almost."

"I thought you said that Belgians make good police dogs," I reminded her. I thought I had her on that one.

"Well, they do," said Kay. "Wolf could sniff out a police patrol anywhere!"

FOLLOW-UP

1. How did Kay make her story sound exciting?

2. What mistake did Wolf make?

3. How do you think Kay felt when she saw what Wolf had done?

The next time you want to send a message, do it big. Here's how. . . .

Flying Messengers

by Paul Langner

From the ground, it looked as if a giant, unseen hand were writing white letters against the blue sky. Actually, the letters were being made by a group of skytypers — five white airplanes with red and blue stripes. The planes, flying at 10,000 feet, were sending out big white clouds at exactly timed moments.

This unusual flying circus was founded in 1952 by Mort Arken of New York City. The group was first called Skytypers and was based in Flushing Meadows, New York. Since then, the airplanes have been bought by a company in Milwaukee, Wisconsin. The company uses the planes to write ads. It is the only such ad service in the world.

Mort Arken

There are six airplanes in all. They are old and sometimes stubborn and rattly. But overall, they are sturdy SNJ-2 World War II trainers. They were used to teach Navy pilots how to handle the P-51 Mustangs and the F4U Corsairs. Arken himself learned to fly in such a trainer during World War II.

Arken's pilots, twenty in all, do this work part-time. They all make a living in other ways. Some fly 747's, some teach others to fly, and some fly military airplanes. "They do this more for the fun than for the money," says Arken.

Skytyping, which Arken invented, is different from skywriting. Most people have seen skywriting. In skywriting, a plane will send out a trail of white smoke as it traces the letters of a word. In skytyping, several planes fly together. They send out smoke that forms a pattern of dots. From the ground, the dots form letters.

How is it done? Arken takes his planes up to 10,000 feet. He orders the pilots to make a straight line across. In his command plane, he has a small computer with a tape drive. The tape has a pattern of holes punched into it. The computer reads the holes and sends out radio signals to the other planes. A radio receiver in each plane changes these signals into electric pulses. The pulses open and close certain valves. When the valves open, they feed a special oil mixture into the plane's tail pipe. As the mixture hits the air, it turns into white clouds.

Each letter takes about four seconds to be typed. A message of twenty to twenty-five letters takes about a minute and a half to type. On a crisp, clear day, such messages can be seen by everyone within a circle thirty miles across.

It might seem as if all the pilots had to do was to find their places, fly around, and let the computer do the rest. But it doesn't always work out that way. On one flight, plane No. 3 had problems from the very start. It hesitated in the cold morning air and would not start. It had to be jump-started by using the battery of a car.

Once up in the air, it turned out that No. 3's receiver was broken. Arken had to tell the pilot over the radio when to hit the switch to make smoke. The radio crackled with his orders of "Now, now, now!" At each *now*, the pilot hit the switch and the clouds came out — exactly on time. If more than one plane had turned up with a bad receiver, however, the flight would have been called off. "You could not handle two planes manually," said Arken. "As it was, the constant *now, now* was driving me bananas."

Each plane carries at least sixty-five gallons of the oil mixture. That's about enough for fifty messages. Some planes have spare tanks behind the pilot's seat. Other planes have a spare seat for people who just want to watch.

This is what Mort Arken's pilots see from the cockpit.

Going along on such a flight isn't quite like getting on an airliner. First, you have to wear warm clothes. The cockpit heater doesn't keep you warm; it only keeps you from freezing to death. You also have to wear special overalls that are fireproof. Then there is the harness. This isn't just a seat and shoulder belt. It is a harness that goes around both the arms and the legs.

"That's your parachute harness," explained Sal Manganaro, the pilot of the No. 2 plane. "If you have to bail out, you open the sliding canopy. Then you jump out so you land with both hands on the wing. You won't have to worry about hitting the tail or anything. You'll drop clear. Then you grab this ring, which will open your chute. You pull it straight out from you. You'll just float down."

Manganaro makes his living teaching pilots how to fly small company jets. Those jets have equipment that takes much of the work out of flying. But when Manganaro flies the old trainer, he must use his seat-of-the-pants flying skills. The controls are of the "Armstrong" type — meaning the pilot's arm has to be strong!

Some people might worry about how close the planes fly. The space between wing tips in some cases is as little as twenty feet. But the pilots just smile at that. Only once in a while does worry creep into the radio chatter.

"Not too close, it's pretty bumpy," says Arken at one point during a flight.

"Hurry up, No. 1," says Manganaro as he touches down behind Arken at the airfield.

"Plenty of room, plenty of room," Arken tells Manganaro.

Then comes the clue to something that really concerns the flyers. "Let's dress up the line," says Arken. "There are photographers all over this place."

It is important to look good!

FOLLOW-UP

1. How is skytyping different from skywriting?

2. Sal Manganaro flies two kinds of planes. What are they? How are they different?

3. Do you think that skytyping is a good way to write ads? Why do you think that?

They jump out of the plane.
A minute later, they open their
parachutes. What happens
in between is amazing!

The Golden Knights

by Jan W. Steenblik

Sergeant Dave Rodriguez stands on the tailgate of the big YC-7A Caribou jump plane. He shivers just a little—from the cold, not because he is about to jump 12,500 feet. He is one of the Golden Knights, a parachute team with the United States Army. He has made more than 2,000 jumps.

Rodriguez steps off into the thin, cold air. In his left hand, he holds a thick wooden baton. His right hand pulls a cord that lets out a thick plume of bright red smoke. The smoke pours from a can that is strapped to his boot. Without the smoke trail, the crowd watching from two miles below might not see him jump.

A split second later, Sergeant Randy Matthews pops his smoke and dives after his teammate. He skillfully moves his arms, hands, and legs to control the speed and angle of his fall. Matthews swoops down to Rodriguez and grabs the other end of the baton.

Now each skydiver bends one leg. They spin like a pinwheel, dropping down through the sky at 120 miles per hour. Their twin smoke trails twist in and out. At 5,000 feet, Rodriguez lets go of the baton. The two jumpers fly apart and pull their ripcords. Three seconds later, their black and gold parachutes open up with a rumbling sound. The two Knights steer their gliding parachutes down. They land right in front of the crowd — on tiptoe.

Founded in 1959, the Golden Knights are the best precision parachuting team in the world. They have shown their skydiving skills in all 50 states and in 31 countries. They have performed at events ranging from air shows to the opening of the 1980 Winter Olympics.

In good weather, the Knights make all their show jumps from 12,500 feet. That way, they can fall for about 60 seconds before they have to pull their ripcords.

Their show starts with the baton-pass jump. The second jump — called the cutaway — is just as thrilling to watch as the baton pass. In this stunt, one jumper falls to 9,000 feet and then opens the main parachute. Soon after it opens, the parachute collapses and is let go. The jumper falls again and then opens a second chute.

The third jump — called the diamond track — is the trickiest. Two Golden Knights jump at the same time. One turns left, the other right. They hold their arms at their sides and their legs straight behind them. They fall at a steep angle across the sky, away from each other. They look like 180-mile-per-hour flying squirrels. At 7,500 feet, they turn back toward each other. The jumpers' smoke trails make a shape like a baseball diamond.

The fourth and final jump requires four Knights.

Three Knights and their team leader move in freefall to make a tight diamond formation. As they pass through 3,500 feet, they suddenly go off in four directions. Their trails make a "star burst" in the sky.

Back on the ground, they are surrounded by wide-eyed admirers. People press close to get their signatures and ask questions. One of the hardest questions to answer is, What does it feel like?

The Knights give good answers. "It's kind of like swimming . . . or floating on a water bed. . . . And it's loud. The wind makes a lot of noise because we fall so fast. . . . It's like being Superman. . . . " Sometimes, one of them gets a faraway look. It is the look of someone who has been asked the question, How does it feel to be free?

Using a Catalog

You can order almost anything from catalogs—records, clothes, even earthworms! Why do people use catalogs? There are many reasons. Some people don't have the time to go to a store to shop. Others live far away from the stores where they would like to shop. Still other people want to buy special items that are not found in most department stores. For all of those people, it is quicker and easier to order things from a catalog. Sometimes there is another good reason to shop by catalog. An item in a catalog may cost less than the same item in a store.

There are many kinds of catalogs, some small and some large. Most large catalogs have three important parts—the index, the entries, and the order form. The **index** tells you on what page of the catalog you can find the **entry** for an item. The entry tells you all about the item. It gives you information such as size, color, and price. Once you have found exactly what you want, you fill out the **order form.** The order form will help make sure that you get the item you want and not something else.

Using the Index

How do you find an item in the catalog? It could take you a long time to find it by flipping through the pages. There is a better way. Use the catalog index.

The index is an alphabetical list of the items that are in the catalog. It tells you on which page an item can be found. The index may be in the front, middle, or back of a catalog. Usually, though, it is found in the back.

It would be hard to list every single item in the index. So, items that are alike are found under one listing in the index. For example, suppose you want a special make of radio. The index will list only the word *radio*, with a set of page numbers. You would check all of those pages to find your radio.

Sometimes you may have to look in more than one place in the index. Suppose you want to buy a lock for your bicycle. You might first look under the word *bicycle*. If you do not find a bicycle lock listed there, where else could you look? You could look under the word *lock*. In fact, that is where bicycle locks are listed in the sample index on page 121.

As you can see, there are several kinds of locks listed in the sample index. Often, items are grouped together under one common, or key, word. In this case, the key word is *lock*. What other kinds of locks are listed in the sample index?

If you can't find an item in the index right away, don't give up. You should always look under other key words.

L

Lamps 500-502

LIGHTS
    Bicycle 666
    Car. 325
    Patio 940

LOCKS
    Bicycle 665
    Door 817,931
    Garage Door 924,925
    Storm Door 931

Log Carriers 996
Log Splitters 919
Loggers' Boots 403

M

MIRRORS
    Bathroom 150
    Car. 326
    Dresser 110
    Wall 862,863

MITTENS
    Baby 707
    Children's 710
    Ski 790

MOTORCYCLE SUPPLIES
    Bucket Seats 340
    Tires 341
    Windshields 340

Reading the Entry

Before you order an item from a catalog, make sure that it's exactly what you want. How do you do that? First, turn to the page that was listed in the index. Then read the entry *carefully*.

Suppose you want to order a pair of wrist guards for roller-skating. Read the sample entry below. What information does this entry give you? It tells you what the wrist guards are made of and what colors they come in. It also tells you how to choose the correct size. Catalogs often have special charts or directions. Always read the directions carefully. How do you measure your wrist size? What letter should you put on the order form if your wrist is five inches around?

The last two lines of the entry give the catalog numbers and the price. There is one number for red wrist guards and a different number for blue ones. You must copy the catalog number correctly when you are ready to order.

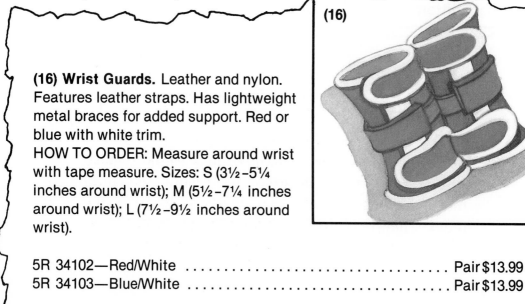

(16) Wrist Guards. Leather and nylon. Features leather straps. Has lightweight metal braces for added support. Red or blue with white trim.
HOW TO ORDER: Measure around wrist with tape measure. Sizes: S (3½–5¼ inches around wrist); M (5½–7¼ inches around wrist); L (7½–9½ inches around wrist).

5R 34102—Red/White . . . . Pair $13.99
5R 34103—Blue/White . . . . Pair $13.99

Filling Out the Order Form

Order forms can look pretty complicated. They have all those lines and boxes! How do you figure out what goes where?

One order form may look very different from another. But all order forms ask you for the same kind of information. Look at the sample order form on page 124. It has been filled out by someone named Cindy Hughes.

At the top of the form are the words *please print*. Why should you print the information instead of writing it? It is usually easier to read something that is printed. If the order form is not readable, your order may not get filled. Or you may not get what you wanted. Your order might even get sent somewhere else!

At the top left, Cindy has printed her name and address. Be sure that you print your *complete* address, including zip code. That will help speed things up.

In the next section, you must tell how you will pay for your order. You should *never* send cash through the mail. Someone could open your order and take the money out. The best way to send money is by writing a check or using a charge card. Ask an adult in your family to take care of this part for you.

The order form will show how to make out the check. Or the adult can fill in the information for the charge card and sign on the line.

The last section to fill out is called "Ordering Information." You must get this information from the catalog entry. If you are ordering more than one item, fill in the information for *one item at a time.* Otherwise, you could become confused.

PLEASE PRINT

Name _Cindy Hughes_

Address _32 Swift Lane_

City _Barton_

State _North Dakota_ Zip _58315_

Phone Number (_701_)_5 2 2_ – _0 0 0 3_

ORDERING INFORMATION

Method of Payment

☑ Check (Make check payable to B. Harris and Company)

☐ Charge Card

☐ ☐ ☐ ☐ ☐ ☐ ☐ ☐ ☐ ☐ ☐ ☐

Account Number

Card Expires   Month ☐☐   Year ☐☐

Cindy Hughes

Customer Signature

Page	Catalog Number	How Many	Color	Size	Name of Item	Price		Total	
301	5 R 3 4 1 0 3	2 Pair	Blue	M	Wrist Guards	$ 13	99	$ 27	98
665	6 H 0 1 1 2 3	1			Bicycle Lock	9	95	9	95
						Total Amount	$ 37	93
						Shipping Charge	3	95
						TOTAL	$ 41	88

As you can see, Cindy has ordered three things — two pairs of wrist guards and one bicycle lock. Read across the first row that Cindy has filled out. On page 301, Cindy found the pair of wrist guards that she wanted. The catalog number for the blue wrist guards is 5R 34103. Cindy ordered two pairs of blue wrist guards, size M. Because the price of *each* pair is $13.99, the total cost for two pairs is 2 x $13.99, or $27.98.

Now look at the second row that Cindy has filled out. On what page did she find the bicycle lock? What is the price of the bicycle lock?

Next, Cindy added all the numbers in the *Total* column. She put that amount in the box labeled "Total Amount." How much does Cindy's total order cost?

Next, Cindy had to figure out how much it would cost to mail these items. Catalogs usually have tables that show shipping charges. You would use the table to figure out the correct amount. Many catalogs have very simple tables. The shipping charges are based on the amount of the order. Look at the shipping table below. How much did Cindy have to add to her order?

Shipping Charge

$10.00 or Less	$2.25	$40.01 – $75.00	$4.95
$10.01 – $25.00	$2.95	$75.01 or More	$5.95
$25.01 – $40.00	$3.95		

The last step is to add the *Total Amount* and *Shipping Charge*. Once that's done, you have completed your order.

Ordering from catalogs can save you time and money. Remember to use the index, read the entry carefully, and fill out the order form correctly. If you do that, you should get just what you wanted.

Questions

1. Look at the index on page 121. How many pages of this catalog have entries for storm-door locks?

2. Look at the entry on page 122. What catalog number would you put on the order form if you wanted red wrist guards?

3. Look at the table on page 125. How much is the shipping charge on an order of $41.50?

Steve and Earl are about to find out that there are some things even tough people can't handle.

Something Really Different

by Walter Dean Myers

Steve's parents have recently adopted Earl. Earl is a street-wise 13-year-old who spent some time in a juvenile center. Now Earl is working with Steve at Micheaux House, a home for older people— "the seniors." One day, Steve gets a phone call. . . .

I got a call at Micheaux House today from my mother. She said that her cousin in the Bronx was hurt in some kind of accident and that she was going to go and see about her. My father was going to take off from work and take her up there. She said that me and Earl should get some pizza or something. Then she would fix dinner when she got home.

Now, when you get a phone call at Micheaux House, you have to tell the seniors who it was, what it was about, and everything. So what happens is this. The seniors think me and Earl should go home and make sure the house is clean — I'm not sure why. Anyway, I got an idea, so I tell Earl and we take off.

This is my idea. Earl and I are going to make dinner. Now, Earl is pretty smart in a way. He can always think of a way to do something so that if you goof up, it won't look so bad. I thought that we should make burgers, because that's pretty easy. But he says no, we should make something that's really different. That way, if we goof it up, no one is going to say that we couldn't even make something that's simple. So we went to the supermarket and looked around for something that was different.

They had rabbits in the meat section, but Earl looked at me like I was strange or something. He said that he didn't eat rabbits. I told him they were like hares and not really rabbits.

"What's the difference between a *what*?"

"A hare."

"Right. What's the difference between a hare and a bunny?"

I couldn't tell him, so that was the end of that idea. Then I had a *great* idea. "Let's get an octopus!" I said.

"A who?"

"An octopus. They got them over here in the frozen fish department."

"You know how to cook an octopus?"

"It's got to be like cooking a fish, I guess," I said. "Cut it up and fry it."

I don't think Earl liked that idea, either. But he said OK, and we bought a frozen octopus. It came in a plastic bag, and we got that and two boxes of frozen green peas.

When we got home, we took the octopus out of the bag. It was so hard that you couldn't even get next to cutting it. We decided to let it thaw. BIG MISTAKE!

We put the octopus on the counter and went to watch a little television. We didn't get much of a chance to be home in the daytime, so it was really cool. Earl said that when he was in the juvenile hall, all they ever did was watch television. I thought that must have been pretty boring, and I told him so.

"It's OK," he said. "You can just look at television and you don't have to think about nothing. Sometimes I used to be glad to get out of bed and just watch television. That way I wouldn't, you know, lay around and think about things."

We talked for about an hour or so while we watched television, mostly about what it was like in juvenile hall. I told Earl it didn't seem so bad to me. He said he didn't think it was so bad either until he found out about some better things. He said, "Think about that!" Now, how can you think about something just because somebody says, "Think about that!"

Then we decided to go out and check on the octopus. Now, this is the truth. Just as we got into the kitchen, the octopus moved. Earl looked at me, and I looked at him. We both kind of took a step backward.

"Hey, man," Earl said, "did that thing move?"

"It looked like it moved to me," I said.

Then it moved again—one of its arms came down real slow. I mean *real slow*.

"I think it's just unfreezing," Earl said. "Why don't you go check it out?"

"Check it out yourself!" I said.

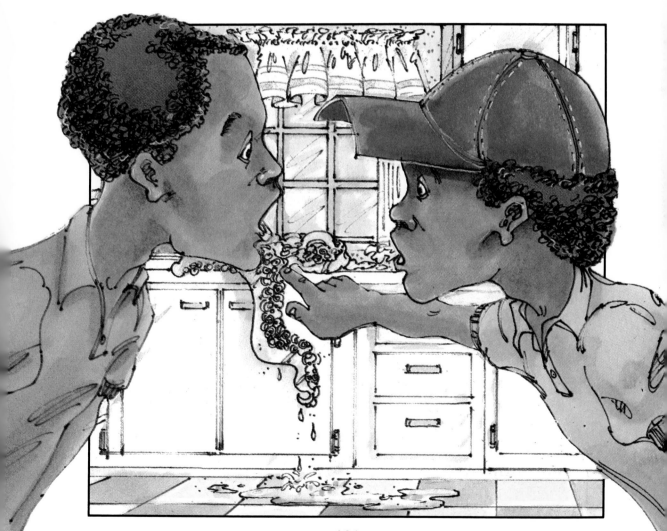

Then we had a meeting and decided that it was probably just unfreezing, like Earl said. But it had just started, so we were going to leave it alone for a while. Then we went in and watched some more television.

We watched one show. Then Earl said I should go and check out the octopus again. Only this time he was smiling a little.

"What you smiling about?" I asked.

"I think you're scared of that thing out there," he said.

"You so brave, you go check it out," I said.

"Come on, man," he said, "we ain't scared of no octopus. We'll both go."

So we both went into the kitchen. This time all the arms were down. It was sitting right in the middle of the counter, looking dead at us. Right then and there I knew that there was no way we were going to cook that octopus. I didn't even want to touch it. Also, I never knew an octopus had a mouth like a bird, but it does. There was only one thing to do — get rid of it before my parents got home.

"Let's put a bag over its head so it won't be looking at us," Earl said.

That was a good idea, so we mapped out a plan. We'd get a big plastic trash bag to throw over it. Then one of us would open the door. The other one would scoop up the octopus and take it out to the trash.

"You grab him," Earl said. "You the oldest."

"You're supposed to be so tough," I said. "You grab him!"

"I can't," Earl said. "I really can't do it. You got to be the man."

I got the plastic bag, and Earl stood near the door.

"When I say *three*, I'm going after him," I said. I wiped my hands on my pants.

"I think his left eye just blinked!" Earl said.

I knew I had to get it over with in a hurry. I took a deep breath, let out a yell, and ran after the octopus. I scooped it up in the bag and ran toward the door just as Earl jerked it open. Wham! Right into my father!

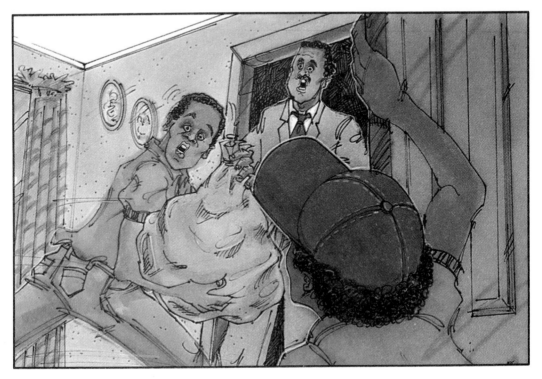

"What are you guys doing?" Dad said, at the top of his voice. "What's in the bag?"

He snatched the bag from me and looked in it. Dude jumped about thirty feet straight up. He dropped the bag and everything. I never knew my father could yell like that. There he was, standing in the middle of the hall and screaming. Earl was lying on the floor, laughing like he was going to bust at any minute. My mother had just gotten to the top of the stairs. She was standing there, trying to figure out what this slimy thing lying in front of her door was.

Even after we had ordered out for a pizza and everything had been explained, my father was *still* mad.

FOLLOW-UP

1. Why did Steve and Earl change their minds about cooking the octopus?

2. Who do you think was more afraid of the octopus — Steve or Earl? Why do you think that?

No one believed the big man could raise a ghost. But then strange things — *very* strange things — began to happen.

Spirit Weather

Based on a story by Jack Tracy

No, I don't believe in ghosts. No such things. And I say this, even though I had an experience that would send you shrieking beneath the bedcovers — a real ghost story. Do you want to hear it?

I was a young man at the time. The year was 1851—fifty-five years ago. I had left my Illinois home and joined a wagon train that was headed for California, to find gold.

By the time we reached the Rocky Mountains, our
food had run out. One day I went out alone to hunt.
I found nothing the whole day. I was just turning
back when I was caught in a fierce thunderstorm. It
blew up out of nowhere. The wind raged, and the
lightning crashed about my ears. The freezing rain
lashed at me sideways. The best I could do was hud-
dle behind a rock.

Once the storm passed, it was dark and I was lost.
The night closed in. Another storm came howling
through and drenched me again. I was weak from
hunger and terror. I was sure the end was near,
when I saw a light. I stumbled toward it.

The place turned out to be a trading post, full of lost travelers like myself. There was a big man there with a full black beard. He had pale gray eyes that you could hardly turn away from. He told me he was a trapper for the North American Fur Company. He made room for me near the fire.

Everyone sat around the fireplace. The talk soon turned to the storm and the fearful weather of the Rockies. "Spirit weather," said someone.

"True enough," spoke up a young man. "If there are spirits in the world, they were around for that storm."

"You're wrong," said the big, bearded trapper suddenly. We all looked at him in surprise. "The true spirit prefers air that is still," the big man said calmly. "And it is all the more terrible for that."

There was a moment of silence. Then the boy — he was no more than sixteen — burst out laughing. "Well, well," he cried. "Do spirits make themselves known to you personally?"

"You're young," said the big man. "You don't know what you're talking about."

The boy jumped up and pointed a finger at the trapper. "I'll make you pay for that remark!" he shouted.

"Easy, son," said one man. "He's three times your size."

"I'm no more afraid of him than of his silly ghosts!" spat out the boy.

"I do not care if you fear me or not," said the big man in his quiet way. "But I have had a lifetime of experience with the spirits of the dead. And I know that you should not make fun of them."

"All right, then!" cried the boy. "Will you set your spirits on me? *Can* you?"

"Yes, I have that power," said the trapper.

The boy gave out a short laugh. He took a money bag from his shirt and threw it on the floor. "There's five dollars! It's all the money I've got in the world. And it says you're a liar!"

The trapper didn't touch the money, but he got to his feet. "I have no money," he said. "But my bear and fox furs are on that shelf over there." He pointed to a large sack on a shelf across the room. "They're worth at least thirty dollars," the trapper said. "Can you match that?"

"Five is all I got," said the boy.

The trapper shrugged. "Then there is no bet," he said. And he sat down.

I thought the big man was trying to bluff his way out of the bet. I was annoyed. "Do you really think you can raise a ghost?" I asked him.

"I have that power," he repeated. "The spirits of the dead seek me."

I didn't believe him. "I'll take ten dollars of that bet," I said. I counted out two five-dollar gold pieces of my own. I showed them around.

"Here," said someone. "I'll cover three more."

"Another three," said someone else. In less than a minute, we had matched the value of the furs.

"Give the money to the boy," ordered the trapper. "I want him to hand it to me himself — when he admits he is afraid to meet the spirit I will send him."

We all followed the trapper into the blacksmith's shack out back. We looked over the place and agreed that nothing seemed to be out of order. Then the trapper placed a pencil and a scrap of paper on a table and led the rest of us outside. The boy was left inside. The trapper shut the door. As it closed, the boy was standing with hands on hips, smiling.

We stood for a moment under the moonlit sky. Then, without warning, the trapper's eyes rolled back in his head. He raised his hands above his head, bent at the wrists. His fingers were hooked like claws. He began to chant in a low voice. It was a real language. At least it sounded like one. But to this day, I can't name it.

After a few minutes, the trapper spoke again in English. His eyes were still rolled back in his head. "What do you see?" he called out.

We heard the boy answer from inside the shed. "There's a white mist forming inside here, up by the window."

I told myself it was the glow of the moonlight.

"Does it alarm you?" the trapper called out to the boy.

"No, not at all," the boy answered in a calm voice.

The trapper began to chant again. He stopped. "What do you see?" he demanded.

Again the boy answered in a steady voice. "The mist is taking on form — the shape of a man. . . . Why, it's Bud Wood, who died of sickness not five weeks back. He's wearing his checked pants and the blanket we buried him in. It's still wrapped around him."

"Are you afraid of the spirit?" asked the big man.

"No," the boy said quickly. "Why should I be afraid of Bud Wood? He was my friend."

The trapper seemed to smile and began chanting again. His hands were still hooked like claws. His eyeballs were still rolled back. We all stood there, unable to move. The cold mountain air tickled the back of my neck.

Suddenly, there was a rattle and a thump from inside the shed. "What do you see?" called the trapper.

"He's moved now," answered the boy. "He's at the table. He's written something on the paper. Now he . . . he . . . "

"Are you afraid?"

"No!" cried out the boy.

Well, *I* was afraid. My heart was banging inside my chest. Every man's mouth was standing open, his eyes bugging out of his head.

The trapper cried out again in that strange language. Then he howled, *"What do you see?"*

"He's coming toward me," the boy answered.

I could hear the thing breathing! I could hear the steady hiss of its breath, in and out, in and out. Those long sighs could not be made by any *living* thing.

"He stands before me," said the boy. "He is taking off the blanket now to show . . . his face. . . . " The boy let out a scream of terror that stood my hair on end. There was a battering on the door from inside. We heard the boy crying, "Don't touch me, don't touch me, don't *touch* me!" There was a long, high scream, then a low moan, a crash, and silence.

We had stood frozen with horror. But now we threw ourselves upon the door and tore it open. Inside, we found the boy lying on the dirt floor. On the table was the piece of paper with the shaky signature *Wm Wood*.

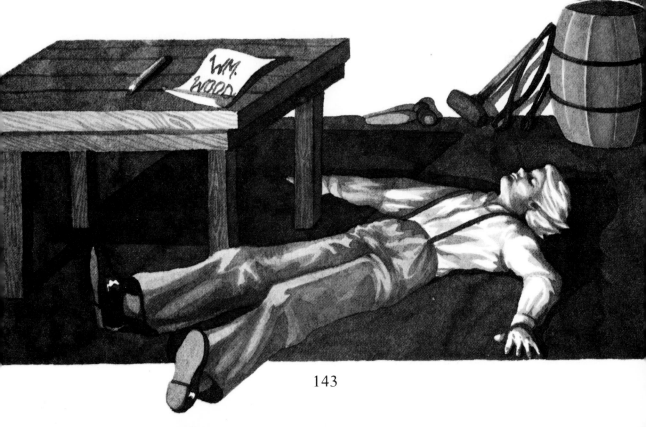

We carried the boy back to the trading post. There, on the rug, he came to himself. He rose up, breathing hard. His eyes were wild. "Where is he?" were the first words he spoke. "Where's that big trapper?"

We all looked about, but the trapper was nowhere to be seen. No one could recall seeing him come inside. Two of us were going to look for him, but the boy stopped us. "No, no!" he called wildly. "He's won his bet! Let it go!" He yanked the money bag out of his shirt and flung it upon the table. "There!" he shrieked. "Take it for him. Take it all! Stay away! Leave me alone!" And he burst out the front door, leaving us standing there in confusion. Within seconds, we heard hoofbeats fading away into the still night.

Time passed as we waited for the trapper to return and claim his winnings. Then someone opened the bag. It was filled with worthless scraps of iron.

The furs in the trapper's sack turned out to be worthless old blankets. Then we searched the blacksmith's shed again. We found the bellows that the boy had used to make that ghostly wheezing sound. Those two had certainly put on a good show.

They also had made off with twenty-five dollars. Ten of them were mine. But they left me with an experience I could learn from, and cheap at the price. I have since become the richest man in San Francisco. No, I don't believe in ghosts. And I never will.

FOLLOW-UP

1. As far as the men outside knew, strange events happened after the boy went into the shack. What were they?

2. How did the boy and the trapper make the others believe that there really was a ghost in the shack?

3. What lesson did the storyteller learn from this experience?

146

How would it feel to be alone — *really* alone?

The Last Man

by Thomas Gunning

Sometime before the sun came up on August 29, 1911, a strange-looking man wandered into the yard of a slaughterhouse near Oroville, California. Dogs barked at the man, but he was too tired and too weak to drive them off.

The barking shattered the stillness and awakened the workers at the place. When they went outside to quiet the dogs, they could hardly believe their eyes. A man who was nearly fifty years old was huddled up against a fence. He wore no shoes or hat. He was wearing only a large canvas rag that had once been part of a covered wagon. His short, thick black hair had been burned off close to his scalp. Pieces of deer hide were stuck through his ear lobes.

The workers could see that the man was very weak from hunger. They also saw that he couldn't understand a word that was said to him. Excitedly, they called the sheriff in Oroville about the "wild man."

When the sheriff came, he saw right away that the man was an American Indian. Not knowing what else to do, he took the man to Oroville and put him in a jail cell. At least the man would be protected from curious people. Food was offered to the man, but he would neither eat nor sleep. He seemed to be afraid that the people would kill him unless he stayed awake to watch them.

Meanwhile, a young scientist from the University of California read about the man in a newspaper. Thomas Waterman knew a lot about American Indian languages. He thought he might be able to talk to the man. He went to Oroville, carrying with him a list of words.

In the jail cell, Waterman sat down next to the man. He began to say word after word, looking for a sign that the man understood. The man listened, but he looked puzzled. He understood none of the words. And then Waterman said the word *siwini*, which means "yellow pine." The man's face lit up. "Siwini! Siwini!" It was a word that he knew.

Now Waterman knew that this man was from a small group of people called Yahi. The Yahi had lived in the hills of northern California for thousands of years. It was believed that all the Yahi had either died or been killed years before. But here, sitting in Oroville's jail, was the last Yahi.

Who was he? Waterman knew that the Yahi believed each person's name was very special. They would never speak the name openly. So, Waterman never asked the man. He simply called him *Ishi*, which means "man."

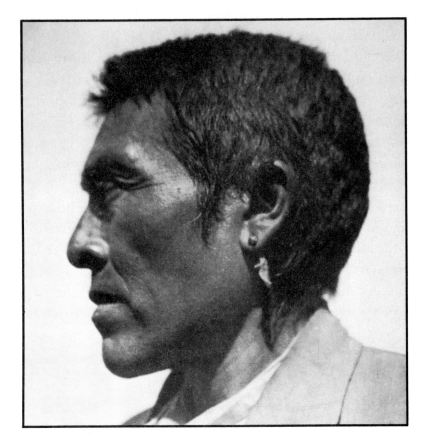

Ishi went back to San Francisco with Waterman. For Ishi, it was like going to another world. With the Yahi, Ishi had lived as people did thousands of years before. Now he was in a strange place where there were many strange things — trains, cars, buildings, and concrete. The city was also frightening for Ishi. Never had he seen so many white people! For all of his life, he had looked on them as his enemies. After all, he knew that white people had killed many of his own people. Seeing hundreds and even thousands of them in one place was almost too much for Ishi.

Ishi was given a room at the museum where Waterman worked. He adapted to his new life as well as he could. On Sunday afternoons, he would show visitors how Yahi tools were made and used. Later on, he was given the paid job of helping to keep the museum clean. This was important to Ishi, for he had always been independent. Ishi also spent his time helping Waterman and others piece together the story of the last days of the Yahi.

That story really started with the Gold Rush in 1849. Gold had been found that year, and thousands of settlers began to pour into California. By 1872, most Yahi and their neighbors had been killed or had died of disease brought by the settlers. Their land had been invaded and taken. Their game had been

Ishi's arrows

chased off or killed. The Yahi were forced to raid settlers' ranches and wagons just to stay alive.

By the time Ishi was born, only a few Yahi were left. In his whole lifetime, Ishi knew only forty or fifty people. By the time he was an adult, there were only four other Yahi left — his mother, a sister, a young man, and an old man. These last Yahi went into hiding. They had always been quick, alert, and skillfull hunters, so they knew how to hide well. They built their last village on a ledge in a canyon, five hundred feet above a creek. It was almost completely hidden from sight. For twelve whole years, no one knew that they were there.

Then, in 1908, workers from a power company were scouting around the creek. They were looking for a place to build a dam. In their search, they stumbled on the Yahi village. They did not see Ishi escape, but they spotted Ishi's sister and the old man as they ran into the thick brush of the canyon.

When the men searched the village, they found Ishi's mother. She had been too sick to run away, so the others had tried to hide her under some skins. The workers did not hurt her. But for some unknown reason, they took all the food and tools that were in the village. One of the workers felt so bad that he returned the next day, but the village was completely empty. Ishi had come back for his mother.

Soon after that, Ishi's mother died. Ishi searched and searched for the others, but he never found them. He was sure that they were dead.

Now Ishi was completely alone. In a way, he was more alone than any person had ever been before. He had watched his people die out. Now there was no one to be with or to talk to.

Somehow, Ishi kept himself alive for three years. But then, weak with hunger and sick of being alone, he made his way into the white people's world. He was afraid that they might kill him, but what else could he do?

In a way, Ishi's fears came true. After three years at the museum, he came down with a cold. In time, the cold brought on TB, a sickness that the white settlers had brought to America. Ishi died on March 25, 1916. He died the way he had lived, quietly and bravely.

Those who had known Ishi were deeply saddened by his death. He had been a cheerful, patient man who loved to joke and talk with his friends. But there was an even greater reason to be sad. Ishi was the last of his people. With Ishi gone, the Yahi were no more.

FOLLOW-UP

1. The title of this story is "The Last Man." Why was Ishi called the last man?

2. Ishi could have gone on living by himself, but he chose to enter the white people's world. Why was that a very hard choice for Ishi?

What if you could go back in time — say, 20,000 years? What would you find?

The Gentle People

Going back in time—that sounds like science fiction. But in 1971, a man named Manuel Elizalde, Jr., did take such a trip. Instead of using a time machine, though, he used a helicopter. He flew to the edge of a tropical rain forest in the Philippines. On the edge of the rain forest stood a group of people who called themselves *Tasaday*. They were gentle, shy people who had never seen anyone from the modern world before.

Elizalde was amazed. He had worked with many of the native peoples of the Philippines. But he had never met any people like the Tasaday.

Where do the Tasaday live?

How could human beings living today not know *any-thing* about the modern world? There are only a few places on earth that haven't been explored or settled. This tropical rain forest is one of them. If you were to fly overhead, you would see an unbroken stretch of blue-green treetops. Some of the trees in this forest grow to be 200 feet tall. That's about as tall as a 20-story building!

The forest is thick with trees, swinging vines, and other plants. The forest floor is a soft mat of rotting leaves and plants. Inside the forest, it is warm and very humid.

Very few people from nearby villages had ever dared to wander into the forest. One local hunter did, however. He met a shy forest people off and on for a few years. Finally, in June 1971, he asked them to come out of their forest to meet Manuel Elizalde.

Why were the Tasaday so special?

There are several things that made the Tasaday different from any other group of people on this planet. The Tasaday did not hunt animals. They did not plant and harvest crops, either. They collected all their food—small frogs, tadpoles, crabs, fish, and fruits. Their stone and wood tools were like those used in the Stone Age—the very early stage of human history. The Tasaday did not build shelters; they lived high up in limestone caves. They made their clothes from the leaves of plants. In all of these ways, they were like people who lived many thousands of years ago.

Something else set the Tasaday apart, something even more surprising than stone tools and caves. These gentle people had no weapons. They had no word for *war*, *killing*, or *anger*. Owning things didn't mean much to the Tasaday, either. They shared whatever tools and food they had. They took only what they needed. When they were offered steel knives as a gift, each Tasaday took only one knife. They seemed puzzled by the gift of extra knives.

What is in the future for the Tasaday?

Meeting people from the outside world changed life for the Tasaday, of course. They now have steel knives, which they use as tools, not weapons. They have learned to trap animals and smoke the meat. They have cloth to replace their clothes made from leaves. They have received some medical treatment. And they have seen modern tools like tape recorders and cameras.

Should the Tasaday be brought completely into the modern world? No, says Manuel Elizalde. They are a people who live a happy, peaceful life. There is no stress or violence — and it should stay that way.

Manuel Elizalde is perhaps the one outsider who knows the Tasaday the best and has worked the hardest to protect them. Through his efforts, the Philippine government in 1972 agreed to set aside the Tasadays' land. It would be theirs alone, to live on as they always had.

Never Shall I Leave

by Nancy Wood

Never shall I leave the places that I love;
Never shall they go from my heart
Even though my eyes
Are somewhere else.

Stan thought his English
assignment was a waste of time,
until he met Loc.

English
Assignment

by Irene Elmer

"You going to English?" Al said.

"I guess," said Stan. He yawned. "Hope I can keep awake."

"What is a verb?" said Al in a singsong voice. "What is a noun?"

"Sorry," said Stan. "Try someone else."

Al laughed. "I ask you," he said. "What has that stuff got to do with real life?"

"You got me," said Stan. He yawned again.

A bell rang. They started slowly down the hall.

"Hey," said Stan. "Who are you interviewing?"

"What?"

"Wake up. Mrs. Ellis told us to do an interview. Remember? We have to interview somebody and write a paper about it. Who did you get?"

Al grinned. "Oh, I lucked out," he said. "I get to interview Carter."

"Carter! Hey, all right! Did you hear about that last game? You'll have a ball. Hey, ask him how he makes those forty-yard runs."

"It's still a dumb assignment," said Al.

"At least you got somebody halfway interesting to write about," Stan muttered.

"Why? Who did you get?"

Stan looked glum. "Some guy from Vietnam named Loc. A refugee. One of those Vietnamese guys that all hang out together."

"Sounds *real* exciting," said Al.

"I can't stand those guys," said Stan. "They never show up at games. You never see them at rallies. They never go out for sports. They take no interest in real life. Study—that's all they do. Just study, study, study, all the time."

"Does Loc speak English?" asked Al.

"Sort of. He's been in this country for a while." Stan yawned. "I guess that's why I get to interview him instead of one of the other ones."

Stan walked into the room where he was supposed to meet Loc. Only one other person was there. It had to be Loc. "You Loc?" he said. "I'm Stan."

"Hello, Stan," said Loc. For a second, Stan thought Loc was going to try to shake hands. His round face was polite but unsmiling. He wasn't more than five feet tall.

"Well, let's get started on this interview, OK?" said Stan.

They sat down, and Stan took out his list. Mrs. Ellis had told him to make a list of the questions that he was going to ask. Stan had first thought the list was a waste of time. He almost hadn't bothered to make one. Now he was glad he had made the list after all. It gave him something to look at besides Loc. He studied the first question.

"OK, Loc," he said. "How do you like it here in America?"

"I feel lucky that I can come to America," said Loc. After a moment, he added, "But it is hard sometimes." He didn't say anything else.

Stan didn't know what to say next. He waited, hoping that Loc would say something further. Loc didn't say anything.

"Well," said Stan at last, "how do you like it here at school?"

"I feel lucky that I can study here," said Loc. "But again, it is hard sometimes." Loc didn't move. He didn't even blink.

Stan wondered if the guy *ever* relaxed. He thought about Al's interview with Carter. They were probably having a great time right now, talking about football. Finally, he said, "Well, tell me some of the things that are hard about it."

Loc's voice was very polite. "America is very different from my country." After a moment, he added, "And American students are not always friendly."

The empty room was very quiet. Stan stared at Loc and thought, "Thanks a lot, you jerk! Friendly! Look who's talking! You guys are all alike. You never talk to anybody except each other."

There was a sharp edge to Stan's voice when he spoke again. "Gee, that's too bad. So how come you left a great place like Vietnam to come to America?"

For just a second, he thought Loc was going to hit him. Loc's black eyes went cold. His whole body went tense. Very slowly, very politely, he said, "You are wrong. In Vietnam, under the Communists, it is not a great place. It is not a country like your country. Here you have freedom. In Vietnam the people have no freedom at all—not even the freedom to leave."

Loc paused. When he spoke again, his voice was hard. "If you try to leave my country, the police put you in jail. The first time I tried to leave, they caught me. They put me in jail."

Stan didn't move. Loc went on. "I was in jail one month. While I was in jail, the police hurt me. See — there." He opened his hand. The little finger was bent. It looked as if it had been broken and had healed crooked. "The police did that to me because I wanted to leave Vietnam."

Stan stared at the finger. He didn't say anything.

"I was a little boy then," Loc said. "I was only ten. But I knew already that some day I would escape." Loc closed his hand around the bent finger.

"I had to wait a long time. I waited three years. You want to know how I got to your country? I hid in a boat. I was a boat person. You know what that is — a boat person? I tell you. A boat person is a person who wants so much to escape from Vietnam that he leaves everything behind. Even his family. He risks his life just to get out.

"I was on the boat for seven weeks. The boat was an old boat. It kept breaking down. All day the sun shone down on us. We had not much water. For the last ten days we had no food. Pretty soon I am too weak to stand up. I lie on the deck of the boat. All day long, I see things that aren't there.

"There were 93 people in the boat when we left Vietnam," Loc said. "When we arrived in Hong Kong, there were 31." He looked at Stan to see if Stan understood.

"Finally I come to your country, to your school. Now I study. I study to learn English. I study so I can get a job. My mother is still in Vietnam. When I get a job, I save my money. Maybe I can find a way to get my mother out."

Loc stopped talking suddenly. The room was very quiet. Stan wondered why Loc hadn't mentioned his father. Then he remembered something Mrs. Ellis had said: "Remember, Stan, these students have lived through a war. Lots of them have seen members of their families killed. Some of them have seen things that are just too awful to talk about."

Loc pushed his chair back. He stood up. "You ask me what I think of your school. I feel lucky that I can study here. But if I am honest, I have to tell you, I don't understand American students. American students talk all the time about games. I think American students are interested only in games. In my country, students are interested in real life."

Loc looked at Stan for a second. Then he spoke again, choosing his words carefully. "Excuse me," he said. "Forgive my rudeness. But why aren't American students interested in real life?"

Stan didn't run into Loc again for a while. Then one day, he and Al were walking down the hall. Stan saw Loc standing by a row of lockers. He hesitated. Their eyes met. After a second, Stan smiled. Loc looked at him blankly for a moment. Then he smiled back—just a little.

"Is that Loc?" Al asked as they walked away.

"That's him," said Stan.

"You never told me. How did the interview go?"

"OK," answered Stan.

"What did you talk about? His homework?"

Stan didn't answer.

"Did he tell you what he does in *real* life?"

"Sure," Stan said quietly.

"Come on. Those guys don't have a real life."

Stan stopped suddenly. "Shut up," he said. "Just shut up, OK?" He felt like punching Al. Al stared at him.

"Listen," said Stan more quietly. "Listen. Sorry, but that isn't fair. You don't know everything. Some of those guys aren't so bad. You know?"

Al just shrugged. Stan knew that Al didn't understand yet. The two of them turned and silently walked down the hall.

FOLLOW-UP

1. What did Stan learn from Loc about Vietnam?

2. How were Loc's feelings about games different from Stan's?

3. At the end of the story, why did Stan get angry at Al?

What does it feel like
to be hugged by a
gorilla?

Gorilla Showdown

by David Taylor

Dr. David Taylor is a zoo vet—a doctor who treats wild animals. One of the first places he worked was Belle Vue Zoo in Manchester, England. While he was there, he came to know two playful young gorillas named Jo-Jo and Suzy.

Jo-Jo and Suzy loved being picked up and held. That was easy when they weighed 10 or 20 pounds. But when they reached 70 pounds and wanted to be rocked in someone's arms, it became more of a problem. It was bad enough that the person's arms ached after a while. But the real trouble started when it came time to put the gorilla down. Like spoiled children, Jo-Jo and Suzy didn't like being left alone. They would nip hard and grab hold of clothes with a crushing grip.

At first they were not big enough to make much trouble. But as time went on, they made checkups more and more tricky. To do the checkups, I would go into their pen with Ray Legge, the head of the zoo, and Len, the gorillas' keeper. I might only want to check Jo-Jo's gums or look at his dark, shiny eyes. Or I might want to hear his heart beat.

Before I could do this, though, I had to play a painful knee-slapping game. When I could stand no more, my playmate would wrap himself around me for a hug. He would then settle down happily in my arms. He would loop his arms around my neck. And

he would either poke his fingers into my ear or tangle them in my hair. If I didn't have a free arm, I would ask someone else to get the instrument I needed and put it secretly on the right spot.

When I finished checking Jo-Jo, I had to rid myself of him. That meant passing him to somebody else, most often Len. Neither Jo-Jo nor Suzy minded being traded in this way. They seemed to think that one pair of arms was as good as another. After Ray Legge and I had gone, Len would take the young ape and put it on the floor. As the animal began to fuss and grab for him again, Len would quickly slip out through the door.

That was how it happened at first. But as time went on, Len didn't always make it. He would try to squeeze through the door quickly. But he would always have two, three, or four hairy arms hanging on to his clothes, his arms and legs, or his hair. More and more, he left bits of himself behind. Clearly, the task of ending the day's fun was becoming much harder.

Then one day, when we went in for the usual checkup, Jo-Jo decided on a showdown. He was already beginning to look like a powerful, nearly grown gorilla.

The checkup itself went without any trouble. Jo-Jo hung on to me with a sweet look on his face and sniffed in my ear. Then it was time to leave him.

As soon as I tried to put him down, I felt his grip tighten. He bared his teeth and lost his sweet look.

"You had better take him, as usual," I told Len.

Len moved next to me, and Jo-Jo thought about it. All right, he was ready to move across. So 70 pounds of warm and hairy gorilla slipped smoothly from my arms into Len's. As usual, Ray Legge and I left the room. Then Len backed off toward the door. Once there, he tried to pick off the ape. But Jo-Jo's

hold either got tighter or it was simply moved to another part of Len's body. As soon as Len picked one
hairy hand off his shoulder, a foot or a pair of strong
jaws would take its place. Jo-Jo dug in, but not quite
hard enough to break the skin.

Len struggled and coaxed. Bits of grapes and
bananas were brought out. But Jo-Jo was not about
to be bought off. If Len was leaving the room, so was
Jo-Jo.

"Let me have a go with him," said Ray Legge.
"Perhaps he'll let me put him down. Anyway, I'm a
bit more nimble than you, Len."

Ray went back in. Yes, Jo-Jo was quite happy
about another change. The sweet look returned to
his face as he turned his interest to Ray. Ray moved
with his heavy load until he was just inside the door.
He cooed softly and petted Jo-Jo's head with one
hand. He tried to loosen the ape's hold with his other
hand. Nothing doing. Jo-Jo stuck like glue. He pre-
tended to be napping peacefully, but his iron-hard
black nails dug into Ray's clothes. I swear he was
peeking out between his closed lids.

Half an hour went by, and it was time to try another change. Matt Kelly, the head keeper, was called
in. Jo-Jo went to him like a lamb. When Matt tried to
put Jo-Jo down, however, he lost some hair, a
pocket, and all the buttons on his shirt. He did not
lose the gorilla.

Now I wasn't sure what to do. Handing the gorilla from one person to another was easy. But at this rate, we would soon run out of gorilla holders.

A sleeping drug seemed to be the answer. I knew, though, that the prick of a needle might make Jo-Jo angry. He might take it out on the person holding him before he dropped off to sleep. I knew, too, that gorillas can bite hard and rip things to pieces with their fingers. We would have to do it without causing even the tiniest bit of pain.

That meant the only way to give the drug was by mouth. In the room where the food was kept, I put a knock-out amount of sleeping drug into a banana, peel and all. Jo-Jo likes to peel his own bananas.

Now, there is a rule about giving drugged bananas to apes. Always offer first a clean, undrugged banana. Having gained the animal's trust with number one banana, you then do the dirty work on number two banana.

With this in mind, I offered a clean banana to Jo-Jo. He took it and peeled it with one hand and his teeth. The other hand was keeping its hold on Matt's right ear. Jo-Jo ate the banana with great enjoyment. He licked the skin and threw it down.

Now I brought out the drugged banana. Again, Jo-Jo took it, peeled it, and got ready to pop it into his mouth. Then he paused. Maybe deep down inside,

Jo-Jo had a generous thought. Or, more likely, he had a feeling—a tiny feeling—that something wasn't quite right. With a gentle pouting of his lips and a soft cooing sound, Jo-Jo rammed the banana between Matt's lips. Matt spluttered and gulped, but Jo-Jo really wanted Matt to have that banana.

I was stunned. If Matt swallowed the drugged banana, it would knock him out in ten minutes. Worse yet, he might suffer for days from the strange side effects that happen to people who have had the drug.

"Spit it out!" I howled. "Don't swallow any banana, Matt!"

Matt spit for dear life. Jo-Jo seemed quite surprised that Matt wasn't grateful. He tried to poke bits of the mushed banana back between Matt's teeth. Matt puffed and puffed, rolling his eyes at us as we stood watching helplessly. Suzy came over and helped clean up the mess. She picked bits of banana off Jo-Jo's hairy chest. Jo-Jo wouldn't touch the banana, and he wouldn't take any other food.

By now it was getting very late. We tried to help poor Matt by doing another Jo-Jo trade, this time back to Len again. The trade went smoothly. But still Len could not get out of the room without his ape.

At last we decided to leave Len in the gorilla pen. A cozy chair was brought in, and a radio was left

playing outside the door. When Ray Legge went back at midnight, Jo-Jo was still happily in place, and Len was trying to nap. It was 7:00 the following morning before Jo-Jo finally fell into a deep sleep. Len put him gently on the floor, crept out of the room, and locked up the pen.

We have never again gone into the pen with Jo-Jo and Suzy. They are now full-grown. When I need to check them, I use the dart gun and a drug. But we all remember the happy times we had playing with them when they were babies. It's too bad they had to grow up.

FOLLOW-UP

1. Why is this story called "Gorilla Showdown"?

2. What tricks did Dr. Taylor and the others use to try to get out of Jo-Jo's pen?

3. Who do you think really won the showdown — Dr. Taylor or Jo-Jo? Why do you think that?

Be a Smart Shopper: Compare!

Shopping can be confusing. There are so many choices! How do you decide which product to buy?

First of all, don't buy the first thing you look at. It makes good sense to compare one product with another. When you compare, think about three things. First think about **quantity**. How much or what size of the product do you need? Second, think about **price**. How much does each product cost? Finally, think about **quality**. How good is the product?

Quantity and Price

Suppose you go to the supermarket to buy some peanut butter. Look at the three jars of peanut butter on page 179. The quantity, or amount, of peanut butter is printed on each label. NET WT. means "net weight." It tells you how much peanut butter is in the jar. Net weight is given in either standard or metric measure, or sometimes both. *Pound* (LB.) and *ounce* (OZ.) are standard. *Gram* (g) is metric. Look at the labels on the jars. Do they all have the same amount of peanut butter?

The price of each brand of peanut butter is marked on the top of the jar. All these jars have the same net weight. So it's easy to compare the price of

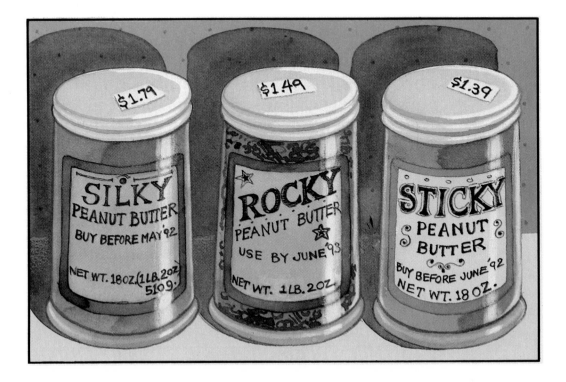

one with the price of another. Which brand costs the least? Which brand costs the most?

What if you are comparing jars of peanut butter that have *different* net weights? How can you tell which jar gives you more for your money? The fastest way is to look at the unit price for each jar. Unit-pricing labels are often shown on the shelf below the product.

Look at the first unit-pricing label on the shelf below. Notice that the brand name Spiffy Peanut Butter is shortened to SPFFY PNUT BUTTER. The retail price shows how much the store is charging for that jar of peanut butter. The retail price is different for each of the three jars. In order to find the best buy, look at the unit price.

In this case, the unit price tells you how much *each pound* of peanut butter costs. The 6-ounce jar costs $2.37 per pound. How much does the 12-ounce jar cost per pound? How much does the 36-ounce jar cost per pound? You can see that the 36-ounce jar is cheaper per pound. It will give you more for your money.

UNIT PRICE	RETAIL PRICE	UNIT PRICE	RETAIL PRICE	UNIT PRICE	RETAIL PRICE
$2.37	$ .89	$1.83	$1.37	$1.73	$3.89
PER POUND	6 OZ.	PER POUND	12 OZ.	PER POUND	36 OZ.
SPFFY PNUT BUTTER		SPFFY PNUT BUTTER		SPFFY PNUT BUTTER	

Whenever you compare products in this way, you should also keep two things in mind.

1. It doesn't always cost less to buy the largest size. Sometimes a store has paid more for the packing and shipping of a larger box. This cost may be added to the price. You can tell if that's the case by checking the unit price.

2. Even though a product is on sale, it may still cost you more than another size. For example, a supermarket might have a sale on the 6-ounce jars of peanut butter. Usually, two of those jars would cost 2 x 89¢, or $1.78. The store is now offering two jars, or 12 ounces in all, for $1.58. So you save 20¢. But you would get the same amount of peanut butter for less money if you bought one 12-ounce jar. That jar costs $1.37. That's 21¢ less than the cost of two jars on sale.

Be aware of this when you use coupons, too. A coupon may save you 20¢ on an item. But that item may still not be as good a buy as a larger size or another brand.

Quality

You have looked at quantity and price. Now think about the quality of a product. How good is it? Before you buy anything, you should always ask yourself certain questions. When do you want to use the item? (Do you want to use it right away, or does it have to last a long time?) How often do you plan to use it? What do you want the product to do? Do you need the very best product, or will another one do?

You can learn about quality by reading labels. Look again at the labels on the jars of peanut butter on page 179. Notice that there is a date on each one. The date tells you what the *shelf life* of a product is. The shelf life tells you how long the product will be at its best. You might not want to buy or use the product after that date. This is very important when you buy goods such as milk and butter, which spoil quickly. Usually, the label will say "Use by" or "Use before" and then list a date. By what date should you use Rocky Peanut Butter?

To judge the quality of a food item, you should also read the list of ingredients on the label. Often, things are added to foods and other products to help them stay fresh longer. If you want to avoid these extra ingredients, you should always read the label carefully.

You can find out a lot about quantity, price, and quality by reading labels. But there are other ways to find out about products, too. Salespeople can be very helpful. Don't hesitate to ask them questions about how something works or the kind of service it needs. Also, check your local library for consumer magazines. They will tell you about the quality of many brand-name products.

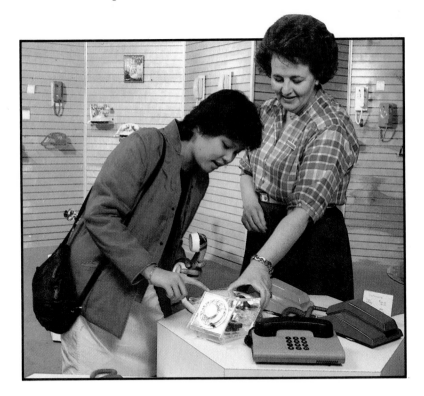

When you want to buy something, remember to compare quantity, price, and quality. This will help make you a smart shopper!

Questions

Use the labels on page 179 and page 180 to answer these questions.

1. What is the smallest amount of Spiffy that you can buy?

2. Suppose three 12-ounce jars of Spiffy are on sale for $3.99. How could you get the same amount of Spiffy Peanut Butter and spend less money?

3. Which of the jars on page 179 has the longest shelf life?

The Brooklyn Bridge has been called a wonder of the world—with good reason.

The Bridge They Said Could Never Be Built

by Marge Blaine

Think what it must have been like to live in Brooklyn and work in Manhattan in the year 1850. On a cold winter morning, you might stand for hours at a ferry dock on the East River. The ferry to Manhattan might never come. It might have been kept back by high tides or chunks of ice in the water. Telephones haven't been invented yet. So you can't call your boss to say you cannot get to work.

For years, people had thought and talked about building a bridge to join Brooklyn and Manhattan. But the East River was wide, and its currents were strong. People believed that a safe bridge just couldn't be built.

On January 23, 1867, a sheet of ice covered the East River.

John Augustus Roebling was an experienced bridge builder who also lived in Brooklyn. In 1857, he drew up plans for a suspension bridge over the East River. People insisted it couldn't be done. But Roebling's experience had taught him that it could. He had just built a suspension railroad bridge —the first of its kind—over the Niagara River. People had said *that* could never be done, either.

The first time Roebling submitted his plans, in 1857, they were turned down. Then, in 1866, Roebling submitted the plans again. They might very well have been turned down again. But the winter of 1866–1867 was one of the coldest ever in New York City. People faced delays in ferry service every day. That was too much. So finally the people of Brooklyn *demanded* that a bridge be built.

On April 16, 1867, a special bill was passed. It set up a company to raise money for the bridge. John Augustus Roebling, of course, would be in charge of the project.

There is an old saying that a life is lost during the building of any bridge. The Brooklyn Bridge was no different. Sadly, the first victim was John Roebling himself. It happened one afternoon in June of 1869. Roebling was standing at the edge of a dock on the Brooklyn side of the river. A ferry hit the dock, crushing John Roebling's toes between two timbers. Although his foot was treated right away, it became infected. He refused any further treatment. Within a month, John Roebling was dead.

Roebling's death might have meant the death of the bridge itself, except for one thing. John's son, Washington A. Roebling, was also a builder of bridges. He had worked with his father on two suspension bridges. He had built other suspension bridges when he served in the Civil War. He was the perfect person to carry on his father's work. For the next fourteen years, he would give all his time and energy to the bridge. In the end, the project would ruin his health.

Bridging the East River was perhaps the greatest challenge any bridge builder had yet faced. Why? There were a number of problems. A firm base had to be built on the sandy bottom of the deep river. The bridge had to be high enough to let the tall-masted clipper ships pass below. And it had to be longer than any suspension bridge ever built.

Washington Roebling knew that one of the hardest tasks would be the first one—building a firm base for two giant towers. To do this, he planned to use two caissons. They looked like huge, upside-down boxes made of iron and wood.

Inside the Brooklyn caisson, some workers dig below. Others climb up the air tubes to the outside.

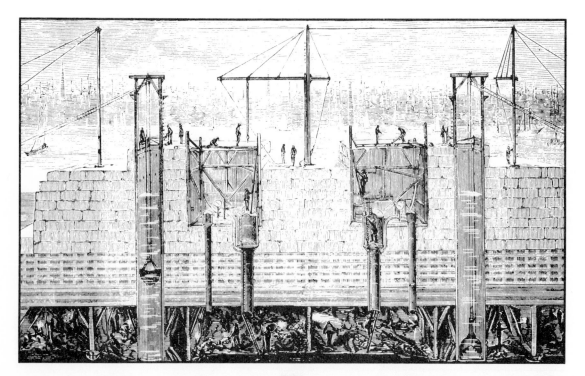

The caissons would sink down to the muddy riverbed. Enough air would be pumped into them to keep water from rushing in through the open bottom. That way, workers could work inside, digging up and hauling away the sand and mud until they reached solid rock. The caissons would then be filled with concrete. The towers, meanwhile, would be built on top of the caissons.

The workers didn't have much trouble when working on the Brooklyn caisson. They reached solid rock at a depth of $44\frac{1}{2}$ feet. But the caisson on the Manhattan side was another matter. As it sank deeper and deeper—50, 60, even 70 feet—more and more workers began to get the bends, or caisson disease.

Anyone who experiences a rapid change in pressure may get the bends. The deeper the workers dug, the more air had to be pumped into the caisson just to keep the water out. That meant the pressure on their bodies was much greater than usual. Before returning to the surface, the workers waited in a room in the caisson. There the pressure was adjusted.

Today we know that a person should spend up to two hours adjusting to the change in pressure. But back then, people believed that five minutes was enough. As a result, some workers felt crippling pains or got dizzy. Some were even blinded for a short time. Roebling himself suffered from caisson disease.

Workers pose on the unfinished Brooklyn tower in 1872.

On April 22, 1872, the first worker died as a result of caisson disease. Another died soon after. Roebling now faced the hardest decision yet: Should he stop at 78½ feet? The caisson had not yet reached solid rock. If the caisson was left resting on sand, it could shift. If that happened, the great tower above it would slip, causing the bridge to fall. But if he didn't stop, more workers might die. After much study, Roebling decided that the packed sand was firm enough to hold the tower. Today we know that he was right. The caisson hasn't moved even one quarter of an inch in over one hundred years!

By the fall of 1872, work on the towers was going smoothly. But by that time, Washington Roebling was suffering greatly from caisson disease. He could not leave his bed.

Luckily, there was another Roebling who was able to take over his duties—Emily Roebling, Washington's wife. She was a strong, lively woman who knew something about building bridges. She traveled back and forth from the work site to the Roeblings' home in Brooklyn. She would talk about any building problems with her husband. She would then return to the work site to relay his orders and make sure they were carried out.

For the next ten years, the people of Manhattan and Brooklyn watched the building of this great bridge. They watched from the shore or from sightseeing boats. Some even dared to walk across the narrow footbridge that had been strung from end to end of the unfinished bridge. At the tops of the towers, the footbridge was almost 300 feet above the water. Some people were so frightened by the great height that they crawled on their hands and knees to get across.

On May 24, 1883, the Brooklyn Bridge was finally opened. The President of the United States, Chester A. Arthur, was there. Washington Roebling, who was still sick in bed, watched through a telescope. Emily stood in for her husband. She waited on the Brooklyn side of the bridge to greet the President. The bridge that so many people feared couldn't be built was at last complete. But that's not the end of the story of the Brooklyn Bridge. . . .

On May 24, 1983, the Brooklyn Bridge was 100 years old and was as sturdy as ever. So the people of New York threw a *huge* birthday party. Over 2,000,000 people took part. There were horse-drawn buggies and people wearing clothes of the 1800's. Boats of all kinds jammed the East River. And, to top it all off, the city staged a half-hour show of fireworks. It was one of the biggest *ever*. In the last $2\frac{1}{2}$ minutes alone, there were 3,600 explosions. That's some birthday party!

FOLLOW-UP

1. How was the building of the Manhattan caisson different from the building of the Brooklyn caisson?

2. Look again at the sentences on page 193. What is the main idea of these sentences?

3. How do you think the people of New York feel about their bridge? Why do you think that?

Long after her diving accident,
Sam still hurt. But it wasn't
her body that hurt. . . .

Sam's Choice

by Harriet Savitz

The golden retriever had no business looking at
her that way. The dog's eyes were warm, hopeful.
Samantha Lee Anderson looked away. She wheeled
over to another cage.

Samantha felt helpless here in the animal shelter.
The sight of the animals trapped in cages really got to
her. She probably wouldn't have come at all this
time. But her mother had needed help in carrying
the boxes of baked goods for the shelter's yearly sale.

Suddenly, Samantha felt that she had to get away
from the eager eyes and the tongues that licked her
fingers. She knew that she would have to pass the
golden retriever again in order to rejoin her mother.

"I'll go right past you," she whispered. She didn't dare look to the side, where the warm brown eyes were watching.

Samantha spun the wheels of her wheelchair faster. She tossed her long, dark hair out of the way as she came to the doorway. But she didn't quite make it. Instead, she came to a halt in front of the retriever's cage.

The dog sat there, quiet and alert. Samantha felt as if she were in a tug-of-war. She knew that she was on the losing side. As she sat there, the retriever squeezed its nose through the cage. It licked her hand, which was resting against the wire door.

"Oh, I see you've met Mandy." It was the woman from the front office. She was now standing by Samantha's side. Sam's mother walked behind her.

The cool, soft nose pressed against Sam's hand. "She's so friendly," Sam said softly.

"Sam, we really have to get back home." Her mother gently pushed the wheelchair away from the cage. Usually, Sam would just give in and let herself be pushed along. Somehow, this past year, it hadn't mattered which way she went. But today was different. She locked her brakes.

"Was she lost?" Sam asked the woman. She looked back at the dog's big eyes. They seemed to be pleading with her. She felt her mother's fingers tapping on the back of the wheelchair.

"No, she wasn't lost," the woman said. Her face softened. "Mandy is a year old. Her owner was a hunter. He took her out hunting one day and discovered that she was afraid of loud noises. The sound of the gun frightened her. So he brought her in to us."

Sam felt her mother's hand on her shoulder. "Honey, Dad will be home soon. I don't want him to have to wait for dinner."

Samantha nodded. She knew how her mother worried. Her father's recent heart attack had changed his life—all of their lives. He needed rest and quiet, but he was always jumping up to do things for her. Would it always have to be that way?

"What's going to happen to the dog?" Sam asked the woman. She kept her brakes locked.

The woman's eyes got dark. She hesitated, trying to avoid the truth. "She's been here about a month now. Usually, dogs like Mandy are adopted right away. Some are trained for blind people. Others are trained for someone like you—you know, to carry things. They're really quite good at fetching books and eyeglasses, almost anything. But with Mandy," she said, "it's her fear of noises that keeps people from adopting her. She would never do well in traffic, with horns honking."

Samantha looked up at the woman. They were both suddenly aware of the small room hidden at the back of the shelter. It was the room where dogs were put to sleep when no one would adopt them.

Samantha fought back the tears. She had not cried for a long time—not after her accident, not in the hospital, not when the wheelchair was brought to her, not even when she knew it was for good. She quickly wiped the tears away and unlocked her brakes. The dog made her feel helpless, and she didn't like that feeling.

Samantha sensed her mother's relief as she wheeled toward the exit. She let her mother guide the chair through the narrow doorway, past the front office, and down the long hill to the car.

Sam's mother opened the front door of the car. As Samantha sat by the open car door, her thoughts raced back to the golden retriever. What if she could teach the dog to carry her books, to bring her things in the house? Then she wouldn't have to ask her mother or her father to do those things. She hated that more than anything—asking for little things.

"Sam . . ." Her mother's voice was worried now. "What is it, honey? Are you sick?" She bent down, facing Samantha.

Sam wasn't sure if she was sick or not. She knew she couldn't leave Mandy behind in the cage. "Mom, I've got to go back and get the dog—Mandy."

"What?" her mother said, surprised. She paused for a moment. "We can't take care of a dog. Certainly not that one. She's so big!"

Samantha shook her head stubbornly. "I'll train her. You'll see. She'll fetch for me and make it so much easier for all of us. Dad and you won't have to keep bringing me the things I forget to take with me." Her mouth was set. She wouldn't give up.

"But who will take care of her? And walk her?"

"I will," said Sam. "If I can't, we'll give her back. I just can't leave without her." Samantha felt her throat tighten. She didn't want to cry now. It seemed unfair to win that way.

Her mother sighed and slammed the car door. She pushed Sam back up the long hill. It was too steep for Sam to have made it by herself. Just this one time, though, she wished that she might have done it without her mother's help.

Sam's mother gave a donation of a few dollars at the front office and filled out the forms. Sam's heart fluttered as they went back to the room with the cages. Mandy still sat there, her head turned their way. She looked as if she had been waiting for them.

One of the helpers opened the cage door and put a collar and leash on the dog. Mandy walked quietly beside the wheelchair as if she had always been there. As they left the shelter, Sam held tightly to the leash. She suddenly felt good about herself again. Mandy was her first big decision in a long time.

Neither Sam nor her mother were ready for what happened next. Sam's mother had been guiding the wheelchair down the steep slope, when a car backfired. It sounded just like a gunshot. Mandy howled and leaped forward. Sam's wheelchair was torn from her mother's grasp. The dog's long legs quickly picked up to a gallop, while Sam held on to the leash.

"Stop! Stop! Please, Mandy. Stop!" Samantha screamed as they rushed down the hill toward heavy traffic. At the bottom of the hill, Mandy hit the curb and then came to a sudden stop. Samantha's wheelchair stopped short, too. The sudden jolt threw her out of the chair and onto the hard earth.

Sam could hear her mother's screams and sensed that people were running to help her. Sam felt Mandy's hot breath on her face. She reached up and locked her arms around the dog.

Hands reached out to help her. But for the first time in many months, Sam refused help. She wanted to be able to choose her own way of getting out of this mess. At last, with Mandy, she had a choice.

"Come on, girl, go, girl. Take me back to the wheelchair. . . . " Sam coaxed the dog. The dog hesitated, then walked a few steps, dragging Sam with her. "Oh, Mandy, it's going to be good. I know it is. It's all going to work out now," she whispered as the dog slowly pulled her back to her wheelchair.

FOLLOW-UP

1. How would having a dog change Sam's life?

2. Why did Sam choose Mandy?

The two thugs said that if
William double-crossed them,
he would never play
basketball again.

The Bribe

by Peter Vilbig

William Collins fluttered a
10-foot jump shot toward the
basket. He watched it fall in
neatly. In less than one hour, the
Bay Arena stands would be full
of roaring fans. After tonight's
game, only one of the two college teams would be going to the
division play-offs.

William looped one more
shot into the basket. His game
was right on the mark. He felt
strong and sure of himself.

As he walked back to the locker room, William saw that he hadn't been alone. Two well-dressed men came over to him from the stands. One was tall, with a thin mustache that barely covered his lip. The other was short and chunky. William didn't like their looks.

"Hello, William," the tall one said. He offered his hand. "You have a minute to talk?"

William didn't take the man's hand. "What do you want?" he asked.

The short man elbowed his partner. "He's going to be unfriendly," he said quickly. "I told you he would be unfriendly."

The tall man saw anger flash in William's eyes. "OK, let's cool down," he said. He spoke in a smooth voice. "We're in business, William. And we have a deal to offer you. We work for a very important man. He wants to make you an offer. It's big money for a small favor, William."

"What's the favor?" William asked coldly.

"OK, William," said the tall man. "You like to be direct. I'll tell you. Our boss doesn't want you to win tonight. He's put a lot of money on the other team. See?"

William had heard enough. "So this is it," he thought. "A payoff. They want me to throw the game." Out loud William said, "Not a chance, mister." He turned and started to walk away.

But before William could take two steps, the tall man grabbed his arm. "Now, I'm going to tell you how it's going to be, William," he said. The smooth, friendly tone was gone. "At the end of this talk, I'm going to put $1,000 in your hand. And you're going to have an off night tonight. You make some shots. Fine. But if the game is close, you shoot bad, real bad. And you do it so nobody knows you're faking. We have ways of hurting your career, William. If you double-cross us, you won't play again. Got it?"

William trembled with rage. The tall man took a bill from his pocket and stuffed it into William's hand. "Be talking with you, kid," he said. Then the two men walked up the ramp past the locker room.

William crumpled the bill in his hand. He looked down the hall. Elaine Powers was heading toward him. She was the sports reporter for the *City News*.

"Well, William," she said, "you were the last person I thought would take a bribe."

"Elaine," William said. He could feel his throat tighten. "You don't understand." How could he explain taking the money?

"Oh yes, I do," Elaine said. "Excuse me, but I have a job to do. I'm covering the game. It could be a very interesting story." With that, Elaine spun on her heel and walked away from him. Feeling trapped, William turned and walked slowly into the locker room.

The crowd roared as William trotted onto the court with his teammates. His heart pounded and his palms were sweaty. He couldn't stop thinking about the bribe. He shook his head and tensed, waiting for the tip-off. Then, in a split second, his team had the ball.

William's first pass was picked off. "Calm down," he told himself. "Think basketball, just basketball." Again, William took the ball over the midcourt line.

He could see a guard covering him to the inside, trying to block him.

All at once, William's mind locked on to the game. It was simple. He had to play basketball. He took two quick steps inside. The guard went for the fake. William moved fast to the outside. He went high in the air. Swish—score!

From that point on, William clicked. By the end of the fourth quarter, it was still too close to call.

Twenty seconds were left on the clock, and the game was tied at 108–108. William had the ball. He held back, letting the clock run down—8, 7, 6, he counted. Outside fake, spin under the basket, and then William was in the open. He went up. His shot rimmed the basket and started to drop away. But another hand shot up and tipped the ball in.

The Arena went wild! Was there time for the other team to score? The clock was running—3, 2 . . . The ball was arcing through the air when the buzzer blared. The ball bounced off the backboard—no basket! Final score, 110–108. William was on his way to the play-offs. He turned from the wildly cheering crowd and headed quickly for the locker room.

Just outside, William saw the two thugs waiting for him. He pulled the $1,000 bill from inside his sock. He hadn't known where else to put it. "I think you dropped this," he said. He stuffed the bill in the tall man's pocket.

"You blew it, buddy," the short one said. His voice sounded ugly. "You're going to pay, too."

"I'll be waiting," William shot back. He walked fast. He dodged through the crowd and went out a back exit. Now, if only he could find Elaine. Outside he yelled at Bill McNalty, another reporter. "Hey, have you seen Elaine?"

"She left with two guys before the game. She said she had a big story. It must have been big, because she acted real nervous."

"What did the guys look like?" William asked.

"One tall, one short," the reporter said.

William grabbed McNalty's arm. "What kind of car does Elaine drive?"

McNalty looked puzzled. "A blue sports car, I think. Hey, what's going on?"

But William was already racing across the lot to the parking spaces for the press. Elaine's car was there, all right.

William looked into the car. Elaine was lying in the back seat. Her hands were tied, and her mouth was taped. William checked all the doors—locked.

Then he checked the windows. One of the rear windows was open a crack. He hooked his fingers over the window and pulled hard. He pulled the window out about three inches. He reached in and unlocked the door. He removed the tape and untied Elaine.

"William," she said, "I thought——"

"I know what you thought," he cut her off.

Voices came to them from the distance. William looked quickly under the car seat and grabbed Elaine's car jack. Then he pulled Elaine out and gently closed the car door. They hid behind a nearby car. The voices got closer.

As the two thugs reached the car, William saw his chance. He jumped, tackling them both at the same time. Elaine made a dash for her two-way radio in the car and called the police. William held off the two startled men with the car jack.

"The police will be here in a minute," she said.

William nodded. "Only problem is, their boss is still free. He could make trouble for us."

"No problem," Elaine said. She grinned and pulled a tiny recorder from her jacket. "When they brought me to the car, they were talking. They figured I'd be out of the way. So they told everything—names, dates, numbers."

Already police sirens split the air. "I hope they get here soon," said Elaine. "I've got a big story to write."

"Right," said William. "And I've got to get some rest. I've got to get ready for the play-offs."

FOLLOW-UP

1. What problem did William face?

2. Why won't the two thugs' boss be able to make trouble for William and Elaine?

3. What do you think Elaine will say about William in her newspaper story?

Foul Shot

by Edwin A. Hoey

With two 60's stuck on the scoreboard
And two seconds hanging on the clock,
The solemn boy in the center of eyes,
Squeezed by silence,
Seeks out the line with his feet,
Soothes his hands along his uniform,
Gently drums the ball against the floor,
Then measures the waiting net,
Raises the ball on his right hand,
Balances it with his left,
Calms it with fingertips,
Breathes,
Crouches,
Waits,
And then through a stretching of stillness,
Nudges it upward.

The ball
Slides up and out,
Lands,
Leans,
Wobbles,
Wavers,
Hesitates,
Exasperates,
Plays it coy
Until every face begs with unsounding screams—

And then,
    And then,
        And then,

Right before ROAR-UP,
Dives down and through.

Most people avoid danger. But Ron Taylor and Eva Cropp go looking for it.

They Work Close to Death

from *Sharks and Shipwrecks* by Hugh Edwards

Ron Taylor: Ron is an award-winning underwater photographer. His work has taken him and his partner-wife, Valerie, to some of the most dangerous and exciting waters in the world.

Here, he tells of his trip in 1970 to South Australia with filmmaker Peter Gimbel. The year before, Peter and his crew had set out to film one of the most dangerous creatures of the sea — the great white shark. They had not found any. But this trip was different. Three great whites were seen from the ship. It was time for Ron Taylor and the others to get to work.

In the underwater cages hanging off our ship, we watched and waited by Dangerous Reef. We strained our eyes to catch the movement of pale torpedo shapes in the underwater gloom. Would the sharks we had seen from the surface come in? Would we get film? Or would they be spooked by the cages?

There was a movement out there, something huge moving in the distance. Then, suddenly, the first white shark appeared with slow strokes of its tail.

"Here he comes!" I said to myself. I felt grateful and relieved. I held the big camera tight against my shoulder and looked along the sights. I pressed the trigger and kept the camera rolling. The shark boldly swerved in, past the two cages. It looked at us with the dark eyes that had seemed more like black holes at a distance.

But there was nothing ugly about the creature. It was magnificent. Its snout was cone-shaped. Its mouth hung open slightly, showing the lower teeth. Every inch a hunter. It was the world's rarest and most dangerous shark. The great white.

The shark turned. Three meters from the cage, it wrinkled its nose, bared its teeth, and opened its mouth wide. I could see the attack coming. I gripped my camera tight. Without slowing down, the shark swam straight up to the cage. I saw the white fangs and, beyond them, the red tunnel of its throat. It was a sight usually seen only by creatures about to die.

Then the shark hit the top float of the cage. If the float had been a seal, the sharp dagger teeth would have made a terrible, slashing wound. Instead, there was just the sickening crunch of teeth on metal.

The shark backed off. It shook its head like a boxer who has taken a sharp left hook. "Is he spooked?" I wondered. "Is this the end of it?"

But the shark was far from through. It came back to mouth the bars all the way down the cage. The screech of teeth on metal sent shivers up the backs of our wet suits.

I was less than an arm's length from the great cone-shaped snout and teeth. I found myself looking at the huge, dark eye. And I wondered what was going on in the brain behind the bullet-shaped nose.

"What are you thinking, shark, about the funny creatures behind the bars? Would you eat us if you could get at us?"

As the shark rolled past, its eye remained fixed on us — like a dog outside a chicken coop. "Hope the cage holds," I thought. It was not all that strong.

In the back of my mind, I wondered what we would do if the shark forced its way through the bars. "Bang him on the nose with a camera, I suppose, and bail out quick," I answered myself. But it wasn't a very convincing thought. The shark would get us if it wanted, before we reached the boat. Also, I knew from experience that nothing would turn away a determined white except death itself.

"There he goes!" I thought. The shark half-rolled, slammed the cage with its tail, and disappeared under the ship.

I checked the camera to see how much film I had left. Then I turned and grinned at the photographers in the other cage. Success at last! The fact that we had waited so many months made it all the sweeter.

Then the shark was back. The same one? No, it was another. And this one, too, went through the same motions. First, it attacked the cages while our cameras ran steadily. Then it finned away to tug and tear at the horse-meat baits that were hanging from the ship and the corners of the cages.

It was better than we had dared hope. Attack, attack, attack. That's the difference between the whites and other sharks. Other sharks are coaxed into biting at the baits. But the whites strike at anything, once they have found blood in the water.

More sharks! They went from the baits to the cage to the ship's hull. They even attacked the rudder and propeller. They mouthed and bit at anything they saw. They kept the same effortless pace the whole time. They never slowed down or hurried.

It was this terrible calm that was, in a way, the most frightening thing about them. Also the fact that they watched us all the time. They noted our every movement with their great, dark eyes, as they swam back and forth, never stopping.

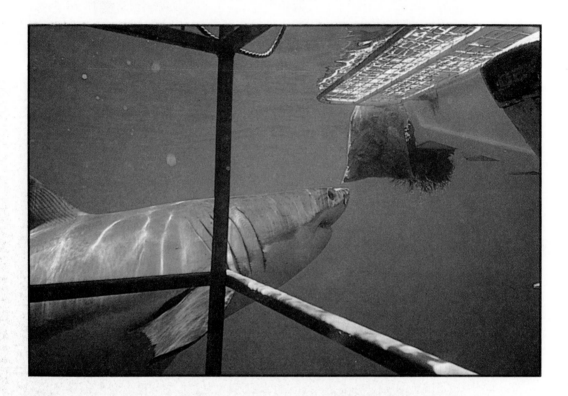

We knew that many of the shark attacks made on divers — and most of the deadly ones — had been by white sharks. Perhaps they mistake the black wet suits and flippers for seals. Who knows? I myself think that a hungry white would attack any large creature.

We also knew that the aluminum cages would not hold up under a really determined attack by a great white. They were built light for easy handling in the water. Of course, the danger made for a better film.

There are bigger whites than the ones we filmed at Dangerous Reef. Those were all males, and it is well known that females grow much bigger. But Peter's film was a truly magnificent film. I can't imagine doing anything better. Still, my mind keeps turning with ideas and plans.

We will be doing more work on white sharks. I'm not sure just what we'll do or how we'll do it. But we'll be doing it. After all, there *is* only one white shark. The most amazing, magnificent, and mightiest of all the sharks in the ocean. The ultimate shark.

Eva Cropp: Eva is a diver who also has worked close to danger. Eva helped diver Ben Cropp film sea snakes that live in the reefs of Australia's Coral Sea. Sea snakes have a poison that is ten times as strong as the poison of a cobra. They eat small fish and other sea creatures. They have few enemies. Perhaps that is why they come right up to divers. Here, Eva tells how she became used to snakes of all kinds, even the deadly sea snake.

In New South Wales, you just get used to snakes after a while. We'd get out a mixing bowl and find a tiger snake coiled up in it. Or we'd be running downhill along a path and find a snake coiled on the track. You couldn't stop, so you just jumped high in the air, and hoped. . . .

Snakes are a fact of life in the bush. So by the time I joined Ben in his underwater filming of sea snakes, I'd had good training.

I must admit the first sea snake I met gave me a bad time. It was while we were making one of Ben's films. He likes a strong reaction in his shots. And he sure got one that time.

The snake swam up to me, quite slowly at first. I thought, "This isn't too bad. What's all the fuss about?" But then it speeded up. I kicked, which made it furious, and it attacked. The more I kicked, the more it darted at me.

When I missed, the snake dodged past my flipper. I was all too aware that I had no wet suit on to protect me. I can still see the snake's head, with beady eyes and forked tongue flicking in front of my mask. After that, I shut my eyes and screamed through my snorkel. They heard me on the boat! And I lashed out blindly with my speargun. When I opened my eyes, the snake was gone. I felt foolish. But it was a good experience; it made me respect sea snakes.

Sea snakes can be grumpy at times. They're the only sea creatures I know that will attack seemingly without reason. Most wild animals will fight if backed into a corner. That's natural. But snakes sometimes seem to look for trouble. We've had them attack divers over and over. They peck the wet suits like angry birds. Luckily, they have only short fangs.

The fangs don't get through the rubber, unless the snake is very large.

Not all of them attack. Perhaps only one in ten, when the snakes are acting bold. And often it's something the diver does that triggers them off. They don't like sudden movements or to be bumped. And a sure way to make them furious is to kick at them with a flipper.

Sea snakes are very curious. They like to crawl around you and explore you — if you can stand it! If you can't, the best way to get rid of them is to block their view with a flipper. You must keep very still. After a time, they get bored and go back to the bottom again.

Of course, I wouldn't kill one, unless it had to be done to save someone's life. I hate killing. I've never been a spearwoman and don't like to see fish speared. I'm much more interested in live animals.

If I could have my wish, I guess I'd be a marine biologist. As it is, I make films on sea creatures with Ben. That's fun, too. Even with sea snakes.

FOLLOW-UP

1. The title of the story is "They Work Close to Death." How is this true of both Ron Taylor and Eva Cropp?

2. Ron and Eva tell how they feel toward the creatures they study. How are their feelings alike?

Glossary

A

a·dapt To change in order to become used to something new: *Most pets could not adapt to living in the wild.*

a·dopt To take someone into one's own family and treat him or her as a member of the family: *They adopted a baby.*

a·larm To frighten; cause fear: *Thunder alarms me.*

a·larmed Frightened; feeling suddenly afraid.

a·lert **1.** Quick to understand things: *A good detective must have an alert mind.* **2.** Watchful; wide-awake: *If the guard had been alert, he would have caught the thief.*

a·lu·mi·num A light-weight, silvery-white metal.

an·noy To bother; make angry: *The dog's barking annoyed me.*

an·noyed Displeased or angry.

arc·ing Traveling in a curve.

ath·lete A person who takes part in sports.

at·ten·dant A person who waits on another person: *This garage has a parking attendant.*

ax·le A rod on which one or more wheels turn.

B

ba·ton A stick such as the one passed in a relay race.

bead·y Small, round, and shining: *The bird has beady eyes.*

bel·lows A tool for pumping air: *I pointed the bellows at the fire and squeezed.*

bill **1.** A piece of legal paper money: *Dad paid for dinner with a twenty-dollar bill.* **2.** A plan for a new law, which is presented to a law-making group for them to act on: *We presented a new bill for the protection of whales.*

blank·ly In a way that doesn't show any feeling: *Eva looked*

Word meanings are adapted from The American Heritage School Dictionary, © 1972, 1977 Houghton Mifflin Company. By permission from The American Heritage School Dictionary.

blankly at me, but I knew she was upset.

blare To make a loud, harsh noise: *The car horns blared.*

blurt To say something suddenly and without thought.

board·walk A walkway along a beach, usually made of wood.

bough A large branch of a tree.

C

can·cel To call off: *They cancelled the game because of the steady rain.*

can·o·py **1.** A roof like the top of a tent, usually held up on posts or poles. **2.** The clear, sliding cover over the cockpit of an airplane.

can·yon A deep, narrow cut in the earth made by running water and having steep cliff walls on both sides.

cap·tive Held by force; not free: *The captive hawk looked helpless in its cage.*

chal·lenge Something that calls for full use of a person's energy or skills: *A 26-mile race is a great challenge, even to very strong runners.*

chant To speak in rhythm, without changing the tone of voice: *The crowd at the baseball game chanted, "We want a hit! We want a hit!"*

coax To try to get someone to do something by gentle urging: *Clare finally coaxed Ted into going to the dance.*

cold Unfriendly: *Jan's cold stare made me nervous.*

col·lapse To fall in suddenly; cave in: *I was too heavy for the chair, and it collapsed.*

com·ic A person who is funny or amusing.

com·pete To take part in a contest or game.

com·pli·ca·ted Not easy to understand: *This game is hard to play because the rules are complicated.*

con·crete A building material made of sand, pebbles, and crushed stone, held together by cement.

con·fused Mixed up: *I reread the directions, but I was still very confused.*

con·fu·sion The condition of being confused, or completely puzzled: *I stared in confusion at the secret message.*

con·stant Over and over again; without stopping: *We had constant rain for the first four days of our trip.*

con·sum·er Someone who buys and uses goods and services.

con·trap·tion Something invented or put together for a certain purpose: *This contraption, made from parts of a bike, goes easily up steep hills.*

con·vince To cause someone to believe or feel certain of something: *He convinced me that his story was true.*

con·vinc·ing **1.** Causing someone to believe something: *Mayor Ellis won many votes because she is such a convincing speaker.* **2.** Believable: *Those fake flowers are so convincing that bees land on them.*

cooed Past tense of *coo*: To make a low, soft sound like a dove: *He cooed to the baby.*

cord·ing A thin rope made of strands twisted together.

coy Pretending to be shy.

cur·rent The steady movement of something, as of water in a river: *The current pulled the boat down the river.*

D

dazed Shocked and unaware of one's surroundings: *She looked dazed and didn't answer me.*

deaf·en·ing Making such a loud noise that one cannot hear for the moment.

death·ly Very: *Martin is deathly afraid of snakes.*

de·sert·ed Having been left by people who have no plans for returning; abandoned: *The deserted house was falling apart.*

de·ter·mined Showing firmness of purpose; having no thought of giving up: *Pat was determined to make the team, and she finally did.*

di·et The usual food eaten by a person or an animal: *The sparrow's diet includes insects and seeds.*

di·rect Saying exactly what one means: *Amy is upset with me because I was direct with her.*

di·vi·sion One of the parts or groups into which something is divided: *Our team plays in the midwest division.*

dodge To avoid by moving quickly aside or out of the way.

do·na·tion Money given as a gift to a person or group.

drench To make very wet.

drift **1.** To be carried along by the movement of water: *The leaves drifted slowly down the stream.* **2.** To move without hurrying: *Maxie drifted over to see what Judy was doing.*

E

ex·as·per·ate To make very angry: *Henry exasperates Jean because he is always late.*

F

faith·ful·ly 1. In a way that shows one is loyal: *Every afternoon, Maury faithfully waited for Kate.* 2. Exactly: *We followed Bill's directions faithfully, but we still got lost.*

fetch To go after something and return with it.

flut·ter To beat quickly: *The bird fluttered its wings.*

foul line In baseball, one of two lines that goes from home plate to the outfield and shows the area in which a fair ball can be hit.

fumes Any smoke or gas that may cause sickness or has an unpleasant smell.

G

gad·get A small tool used for a task: *A can opener is a very useful gadget.*

game Animals, birds, or fish that are hunted for food.

gen·er·ous Willing to give or share; unselfish.

glint To gleam or flash: *Sunlight glinted on the water.*

gloom Darkness; dimness.

glum In low spirits; unhappy.

gos·sip Thoughtless talk, often about things that may have little truth to them: *The gossip was that our teacher was strict, but we thought he was nice.*

grav·i·ty The force that pulls things toward the earth: *Spaceships must travel at great speeds to escape the earth's gravity.*

grump·y Easily annoyed or angered: *Yesterday I felt grumpy and yelled at everybody.*

H

haul To pull, drag, or carry.

head·way Movement forward: *We had a hard time making headway through the crowd.*

heave The act of throwing with great effort: *With one heave, they threw the big box into the truck.*

hes·i·tate To be slow to act, speak, or decide; pause uncertainly.

hu•mid Damp; moist: *After it rains, the air is often humid.*

I

ig•nore To pay no attention to.

in•de•pend•ent Able to live on one's own: *Joanie wanted a job so that she could earn money and be independent.*

in•fect•ed Filled with germs; diseased.

in•flate To blow up by filling with air or another gas: *I inflated the tires on my bike.*

in•gre•di•ents Something added or needed to make a mixture: *You need four ingredients to make these rolls.*

in•stru•ment A tool used by a doctor, a dentist, or a scientist.

in•vade To enter in order to attack, steal, or take over: *The army invaded the tiny country.*

J

jolt A sudden jerk or bump: *The bus stopped with a jolt.*

ju•ve•nile Having to do with young people.

L

lash **1.** To hold tightly in place with rope, cord, straps, etc.: *We lashed the boxes to the roof of the car.* **2.** To strike with force: *The wind blew hard, and the freezing rain lashed my face.*

M

mag•nif•i•cent Grand; remarkable; of great beauty, size, etc.: *As the sun set, it spread magnificent purple, red, and pink colors across the sky.*

make A line of goods; a brand: *Mom has been buying the same make of car for years.*

man•u•al•ly By using one's hands: *Our machine was broken, so we had to do the job manually.*

mer•chant **1.** A person who buys and sells goods for profit: *That merchant charges the highest prices in town.* **2.** Having to do with buying and selling: *The section of town with all the shops is known as Merchant Row.*

N

na•tive Belonging by birth to a certain country: *The best way to learn another language is to stay with the native people.*

na·ture A person's usual mood or way of behaving: *Bobbie has a selfish nature.*

nim·ble Able to move quickly and easily: *Cats are nimble.*

nudge To push gently: *The dog nudged my hand.*

O

out·bound Headed away; going out: *Marcy had to get the outbound bus to go home.*

out·burst A sudden show of strong feeling.

P

pan·ic To feel a sudden, overpowering fear: *Jesse panics whenever he sees a snake.*

pay·off Money given to someone to make him or her act dishonestly; a bribe.

plead To ask for something in a way that shows deep feeling: *She pleaded for help.*

plume Something that looks like a large feather: *A plume of smoke rose from the chimney.*

plum·met To drop straight down: *The hawk plummeted from the sky.*

port **1.** A town having a harbor for ships that pick up and deliver goods. **2.** The left-hand side of a ship as one faces forward.

pout To push out the lips.

prac·ti·cal **1.** Useful; workable: *This table is not beautiful, but it's practical.* **2.** Seeing things as they really are, rather than as one would like them to be: *Jason is very practical; he never sets unreachable goals for himself.*

pre·fer To like better: *I prefer to stay home tonight.*

prod·uct Something made or prepared by machine.

pros·pect·ing Exploring an area for gold, silver, etc.

R

rack·et A loud, long-lasting noise that is unpleasant.

raid To attack suddenly in order to get something: *The seagulls raided our lunch basket.*

ral·ly A large meeting at which people show support for a cause: *All the students came to the basketball rally.*

ram **1.** To force into a small space: *The mail carrier rammed the mail into our mailbox.* **2.** To crash into: *An iceberg rammed the big ship and sank it.*

rap·id   Fast; swift.

ref·u·gee   A person who runs away, often from his or her country, in order to find safety.

re·lay   To send or pass along from one person to another: *Dan relayed the homework assignment to me, and I relayed it to Doreen.*

re·lieved   Feeling a sudden lessening of worry or tension: *She was greatly relieved to find her missing wallet.*

re·quire   To need; call for: *This bread requires four cups of flour and one cup of milk.*

rest·less   Unable to rest, relax, or be still: *She was too restless to go to sleep.*

rim   **1.** The border or edge of something. **2.** To go around the rim of a basket, cup, etc.

rip·cord   A cord that is pulled to let a parachute out of its pack.

rit·u·al   A set of actions that are repeated in exactly the same way, as a usual practice: *Walking the dog around the block is part of Susan's morning ritual.*

S

sea·worth·y   Properly built and equipped for putting to sea: *Our old boat has many leaks, but our new boat is seaworthy.*

se·cu·ri·ty   Anything that makes sure something stays safe or secret: *After the robbery, we put a new bolt lock on the door for security.*

sen·ior   Older person.

serve   **1.** To do a term of duty: *He served in the army.* **2.** To take care of customers; wait on: *Craig served twenty people at dinner.* **3.** To put a ball into play, as in tennis: *In the second game, Jenny served first.*

set·tle·ment   A small, newly formed group of people living in an area: *The settlement was twenty miles from the nearest town.*

shat·ter   **1.** To break something suddenly into many pieces; smash: *The baseball shattered the window.* **2.** To break into suddenly, as with a loud noise: *A loud voice shattered the stillness of the night.*

show·down   An event that forces something to be decided: *The game was a showdown between the two best teams.*

shriek   To make a loud, high-pitched sound.

side effect   An effect, often unpleasant, other than the one that is expected when using a drug.

sig•na•ture The name of a person as written by himself or herself: *I put my signature on the check.*

slaugh•ter•house A building in which animals are killed for meat.

slim•y Slippery and sticky: *Snails leave a slimy trail.*

slunk Past tense of *slink*: To move in a quiet way, so as not to be seen.

snout The long or pointed nose or jaws of an animal.

sol•emn Serious; not joking: *James was solemn as he began his math test.*

soothe To calm: *The soft music soothed me.*

spi•ral Something having the shape of a curve that goes around and around a fixed point; something having the shape of a coil.

splut•ter To make a spitting sound: *The motor spluttered and then stopped completely.*

star•board The right-hand side of a ship as one faces forward.

streak To move at high speed; rush: *The train streaked by.*

stress Something that causes one to feel worried or mentally strained: *Larry couldn't take the stress at work, so he changed jobs.*

struc•ture Something built according to a plan, such as a building or bridge.

stub•born **1.** Unwilling to change one's mind, even for good reasons: *The stubborn child wouldn't eat her dinner.* **2.** Hard to handle or work with: *Nothing grows in this stubborn soil.*

stunned **1.** Unaware of one's surroundings, as a result of a blow; dazed: *The stunned player lay on the field after being hit by the ball.* **2.** Shocked: *I was stunned when I heard the bad news.*

stur•dy Strong and well-built: *I stood on a sturdy chair.*

sub•mit To present something for another person to judge: *I submitted an outline of my paper to the teacher.*

sup•plies Goods that are collected and then given out when needed: *We bought supplies for a camping trip.*

sur•vive **1.** To stay alive: *We learned to survive in the wilderness.* **2.** To live through an event: *I survived the crash.*

swarm   **1.** To move or gather in large numbers: *Fans swarmed onto the football field.* **2.** To be filled or overrun: *The lakes and streams swarmed with fish.*

T

tack·le   **1.** To take on and wrestle with in order to overcome: *Sarah tackled the first problem on the worksheet.* **2.** To grab hold of and throw one's weight against someone in order to stop that person: *Just after William caught the ball, John tackled him.*

ten·ant   A person who pays rent to live in a building owned by someone else.

tense   **1.** Tightly stretched; strained: *His face was tense as he waited for the bad news.* **2.** Causing one to become greatly excited or nervous; suspenseful: *It was a tense game.* **3.** To make or become tense: *The runners tensed as they waited for the sound of the starting gun.*

terms   Conditions: *Both sides agreed to the terms of the peace treaty.*

thaw   To become less stiff by being warmed: *Thaw the frozen chicken before cooking it.*

tor·na·do   A storm with winds that swirl around in a funnel shape at speeds of up to 300 miles per hour.

tor·pe·do   A cigar-shaped underwater bomb that is launched from a ship, plane, or submarine toward a target.

tread water   To move one's hands and feet in such a way that one stays upright in the water.

V

vic·tim   Someone who is harmed or killed by another or by accident, disease, etc.: *The victims of the earthquake were given aid.*

vi·o·lence   Force used against a thing or person in order to ruin or cause harm: *Many people are worried about violence in big cities.*

W

ward off   To keep something from striking; turn something aside: *We used a spray on our arms and legs to ward off biting insects.*

ware·house A large building in which goods to be bought or sold are stored: *The trucks were unloaded at the back of the warehouse.*

wa·ver To move or swing one way and then another in an uncertain or unsteady way: *The dizzy man wavered.*

wheeze To breathe with trouble, making a hoarse whistling sound: *Smoke makes me wheeze.*

Art Credits

Photography

ASSIGNMENT
66, 71 Robert Schoen; 74, 77, 79, 80 Marcus Halevi; 88–89, 90, 92, 95 Ralph Mercer; 160, 163, 164, 167 Paul E. Johnson; 183 Andy Brilliant; 216, 217 Paul E. Johnson.

RESEARCH
34, 36 Arizona Historical Society; 48 Miami Seaquarium; 50 F. Gohier/Photo Researchers; 51 Erich Hoyt; 83 Library of Congress; 84, 85 Historical Pictures Service; 86 Cedar Point; 108, 109, 111, 112 Berl Brechner; 115, 117 U.S. Army Parachute Team Photos; 146, 149, 151 Lowie Museum of Anthropology/ University of California, Berkeley; 154–155 John Nance/Magnum Photos Inc.; 157 John Launois/Black Star; 159 Paul Conklin; 186 *Harper's Weekly;* 188 Rensselaer Polytechnic Institute Archives; 190 Museum of the City of New York; 191 Culver Pictures Inc.; 192 The Granger Collection; 193 *Scientific American*, May 18, 1878; 193 (inset) James Kelly Institute, St. Francis College, Courtesy Donal Holway; 194 Robert Maass; 218–224 Ron and Valerie Taylor; 226 Photoresearchers/ Carl Roessler; 228 Ben Cropp.

Cover: Alex Stuart/The Image Bank

Illustration

Anthony Accardo 6–16; R.J. Blake 17–25; Thomas Colletta 26–33; Shel Silverstein 38; David Watson 39–47; Joel Snyder 52–60; Bill Ogden 61–64; ANCO/ BOSTON 67, 69; Patrick Kernan 98–106; ANCO/BOSTON 121, 124, 125; Larry Tyson 127–134; Julie Haskell Williams 135–145; Richard Joachim 169–177; Sharon Drinkwine 196–205; Ronald Chironna 206–215; Bill Ogden 230–239.